Prepare Your Speech and Presentation

プレゼンテーションで学ぶ英語4技能

Hatsuko Yoshikubo

Reiko Ikeo

Reiko Fujita

Ako Yamagata

Aika Miura

KENKYUSHA

Image acknowledgements
Fotolia.com: p. 16 © cacaroot; p. 21 © dimiRamos; p. 29 © fad82; p.37 © Syda Productions; p. 40 © Madeleine Steinbach; p. 41 © Syndy, © Kazakova Maryia, © sattva, © Holmessu; p. 44 © mtaira; p. 49 © Elnur; p. 58 © jagodka; p. 67 © WavebreakMediaMicro; p. 73 © yoshitaka; p. 80 © milatas; p. 87 © CYCLONEPROJECT; p. 94 © takasu; p. 105 © M-SUR

本書は2008年に南雲堂フェニックスより刊行された『Prepare Your Speech』を改訂したものです。

はしがき

　日本と海外との人の行き来が増え続けている現在、自分の考えを英語で表現する必要性は高まる一方です。プレゼンテーションは、あるトピックについて自身の考えを論理的に構成し、それを文章にして、聴衆の前で発表するという作業です。英語学習においてこれらのプロセスを訓練することは、総合的な英語力の養成に非常に効果的です。

　本書は、最も骨の折れる「原稿を書く」という作業を中心に、プレゼンテーションを行うための準備を、段階を追って具体的に示したものです。実際に教室内でプレゼンテーションを行うことが最終目的ですが、そこに至るまでの語彙学習やリスニングやリーディング、それらを活かしたライティングを行うことで、英語4技能をバランス良く向上させることをねらって作られています。

　トピックのレベルは、身近なものから社会的問題まで多岐にわたっており、レベルに応じて、基本的な説明、より専門的な解説、グラフやチャートを使った解説など、多様な発表の方法を学べるようになっています。また、プレゼンテーションのスタイルも、個人だけではなく、グループによるものやポスタープレゼンテーションなど、幅広く経験できるようになっています。英語に苦手意識を持つ人からかなり自信のある人まで、いろいろな段階の学習者に無理なくプレゼンテーションに取り組んでもらえるものと思います。各ユニットのバラエティ溢れるアクティビティや練習問題は、実際の英語プレゼンテーションの授業現場から生まれたもので、きっと皆さんのお役に立つことでしょう。

　プレゼンテーションは準備や練習に時間がかかります。しかし、試行錯誤と努力の末に、自分の言いたいことを英語で表現できた時の喜びはひとしおです。プレゼンテーションは、英語力を伸ばすだけではなく、人としての成長にもつながっていくと言えるのではないでしょうか。一人でも多くの学習者の皆さんが、英語プレゼンテーションの経験を重ねることで、達成感と自信を得られるようにお手伝いができれば、大変うれしく思います。

　最後になりましたが、本書制作にあたり、校正その他多方面にわたりサポートしてくださった研究社の鈴木美和さん、英文校閲にご尽力いただいた John Heywood さん、素敵なイラストを描いてくださった中嶋麻美さんに心からお礼申し上げます。

2018年8月

著者一同

本書の構成と学び方

1. 本書は 13 のユニットから構成されています。巻頭には、プレゼンテーションの概要を説明した Introduction to Your Speech と、実際のプレゼンテーションで役に立つ表現集 Useful Expressions をまとめてあります。

2. 前半ユニットでは 1〜2 回、後半ユニットでは 2〜3 回の授業時間で、語彙やリスニング、リーディングの練習問題、リサーチなどの準備をして原稿を書くまでの行程を終えられるような構成になっています。

3. ユニット配列は難易度順になっていますが、到達目標や時間数に応じて適したユニットを選んでください。

4. 原稿を書き終わるといよいよプレゼンテーションです。本書では原稿を準備することに重点を置いているため、実際のスピーチスキルについては細かい説明を行っていませんが、6 ページの Three Elements in a Presentation を参考に、アイコンタクト、声の大きさや出し方、姿勢、ジェスチャー、ビジュアルエイドなどの要素に考慮しながらプレゼンテーションをしてみましょう。
   プレゼンテーションに向けての練習は、次のような手順を参考にしてください。
   ① **音読**　声に出して読むことはとても大切です。繰り返し音読することで正確な発音が身につきますし、内容がしっかり頭に入ります。
   ② **録音・録画**　レコーダーで自分の声を録音してみましょう。自分がどのように話しているかがよくわかります。「もうすこしゆっくり、大きな声で話した方がいい」とか「この部分の発音は聞き取りづらいな」といったこともよく理解できるでしょう。スマートフォンなどのビデオカメラ機能を使って録画すると、自分の話し方をさらに客観的に見ることができます。姿勢は良いか、視線が聴衆に向いているか、手や体が不自然に動いていないか、などをチェックしてください。
   ③ **リハーサル**　発表前に家族や友人の前で本番のようにプレゼンテーションを行い、コメントしてもらって、修正できる点があれば本番に活かしましょう。

5. 本番のクラス発表では、巻末の Evaluation form を用いて互いに評価し合いましょう。相互評価は聞き取る力の訓練にもなります。Evaluation form は複数のパターンを用意しましたので、適宜コピーして使って下さい。

6. 本書の音声データ (MP3) は、研究社ウェブサイト (http://www.kenkyusha.co.jp) からダウンロードできます。研究社ウェブサイトのトップページで「音声ダウンロード」をクリックして「音声データダウンロード書籍一覧」のページからダウンロードしてください。

CONTENTS

はしがき 3

本書の構成と学び方 4

Introduction to Your Speech 6

Useful Expressions 9

Unit 1   About Myself 16

Unit 2   My Hero 21

Unit 3   Describing Pictures and Photos 29

Unit 4   Giving Instructions 37

Unit 5   Promoting Places or Products 44

Unit 6   Causes and Effects 49

Unit 7   Comparing Two Things 58

Unit 8   Describing Graphs 67

Unit 9   Graph Analysis 73

Unit 10 Research and Presentation 1: Comparing Two Rival Companies ... 80

Unit 11 Research and Presentation 2: Problems and Solutions 87

Unit 12 Research and Presentation 3: Organ Transplants 94

Unit 13 Pros and Cons of Capital Punishment 105

Evaluation form 113

Introduction to Your Speech

1. Three Elements in a Presentation

All the <u>three elements</u> below are necessary to make an impressive presentation. Make sure to put all these gears in position when you practice your presentation.

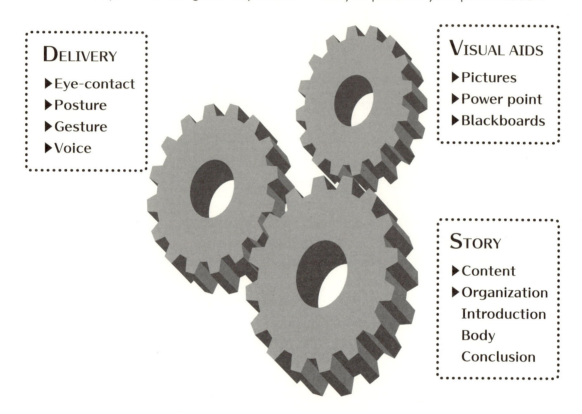

DELIVERY
▶ Eye-contact
▶ Posture
▶ Gesture
▶ Voice

VISUAL AIDS
▶ Pictures
▶ Power point
▶ Blackboards

STORY
▶ Content
▶ Organization
  Introduction
  Body
  Conclusion

DELIVERY: The way you deliver a speech can determine the impression you give to the audience.
▶ **Eye-contact**: Don't just read out from your draft. Make sure you look at your audience directly when you speak.
▶ **Posture & Gesture**: Stand straight facing the audience, but relax at the same time. Try to use gestures where appropriate to attract the audience's attention.
▶ **Voice**: Speak clearly and confidently. Don't speak too fast.

VISUAL AIDS: Use effective visual aids to help your speech.

STORY: Your story must be interesting and attractive for your audience. You need to organize your main points well so that your audience can easily follow your speech.

2. Preparing your draft
Follow these steps to make an interesting and well-organized story.

1) Brainstorming
　始めに、スピーチのテーマに基づいて、様々なアイディアを考えていきます。Brainstorming はその作業のひとつです。以下の図にあるように、まずは中心にテーマを書き、そこから連想されるアイディアをできるだけ書き出します。ここでは Effective presentation をテーマにした例を見てみましょう。

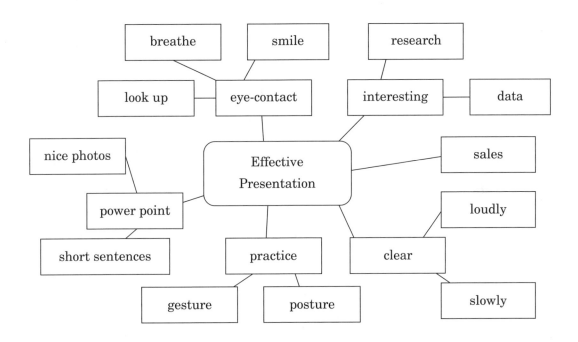

2) Selecting the elements to use
　次に Brainstorming で出てきた様々なアイディアの中から、何が使えるかを考えます。アイディアすべての中から、Topic に沿った具体的なアイディアを選びましょう。必要のないものには斜線を引いて消していきます。

3) Outlining and organization
　使用する要素を選んだら、まずその骨組みである outline を決めます。導入と結論部分は主題のみ簡単に明記し、本文で論じる論点を main ideas としていくつか簡単にまとめていきます。これを土台にして作成したスピーチの構造を organization といいます。

Example of an outline:
- Title: How to make an effective presentation
- 1st Paragraph: <u>Introduction</u> (導入):
    Have you ever made a presentation?
- 2nd Paragraph: <u>Body</u> (本文):
    <u>Main ideas</u>: ① You need to demonstrate good speech skills.
    ② You should use visual materials.
    ③ Your story needs to have attractive contents.
- 3rd Paragraph: <u>Conclusion</u> (結論):
    Three elements are very important for a successful presentation.

Example of good organization:

How to make an effective presentation

Good afternoon, everyone. Have you ever made a presentation in front of many people? The idea of giving a presentation may make you nervous. So, today, I would like to tell you about three important elements to help you make an effective presentation.

First, you need to have good **delivery** skills. Look at your audience and make sure to have eye-contact with each listener. Stand straight and face your audience and smile. Secondly, prepare some **visual aids**. Slides or photos will help your audience understand your message better. Thirdly, try to make your **story** interesting. You could include your personal experience or some related data.

In conclusion, these three elements are very important for a successful presentation. If you keep these three in mind while preparing your speech, I am sure you will make a successful presentation.

Now, it is your turn to prepare your speech. Good luck!

Useful Expressions for Speakers

■ 話者のための英語表現集

1. Greetings　はじめの挨拶

Hello, everyone!	皆さん、こんにちは！
Hi, I'm Kenji. Let me introduce myself.	こんにちは、私は健司です。自己紹介をさせて下さい。
Good morning, ladies and gentlemen, thank you for coming today.	お早うございます。本日はようこそおいで下さいました。
Good afternoon, everyone. I would like to start my presentation.	こんにちは。プレゼンテーションを始めたいと思います。

2. Introduction　導入

Today, I'd like to talk about … / I'd like to speak about…	今日は〜についてお話しします。
These days, I hear people say …	最近、こんなことを耳にします。
Newspapers say …	新聞によりますと
Do you know …? / Have you heard of …?	〜についてご存知ですか？
Have you ever been to …? / Have you ever …?	(〜へ行った) ご経験はありますか？
I'd like to explain … / I'd like to describe … / I'd like to demonstrate …	ご説明 (描写、実演) したいのは
My favorite movie is …	私の好きな映画は〜です。
I'm going to talk about three points.	3つのポイントについてお話します。
After this speech, you will be able to understand …	このスピーチを聴いていただければ、〜についてご理解いただけるでしょう。
This information will help you when you travel abroad.	この情報は〜の時に役立つでしょう。
The purpose of my talk today is to tell you about …	本日の話の目的は、〜についてお話しすることです。
It is my pleasure to tell you about …	皆さんに〜についてお話できて光栄です。

In my presentation today, I am going to report/ show (you) …	本日は～についてご報告いたします。

3. Transition つなぎの言葉

To begin with, / First of all, / To start with,	まず始めに、
First / Second / Third	最初に、二番目に、三番目に、
First / Next / Then	最初に、次に、それから、
Firstly / Next / Lastly	始めに、次に、最後に、
I'll start by explaining …	まず～から説明します。
Finally,	最後に
After that,	それに続きまして、
Now, I will talk about … / Now, I will explain …	それではこれから～についてお話(説明)します。
Now, let's look at …	さて、～について見てみましょう。
Now, let me move to the next point.	さて、次のポイントに入りましょう。
Now, let me go on to the next topic.	さて、次のトピックに移ります。
Overall, / As a whole,	全体的に見て

4. Making Suggestions 提案

It is a good idea to …	～するのはいい考えだと思います。
I think we should …	～するべきではと考えます。
I'd like to suggest that we …	～することを提案します。
I propose …	～を提案します。

5. Addition 追加

In addition,	加えて、
I'd like to add one more thing.	もう一点付け加えさせて下さい。
and what is more,	おまけに、その上に、またそれだけでなく
Furthermore,	なお、そのうえ、さらに、
Moreover,	そのうえ、さらに、加えて　(前文よりもより重要な情報をつけ加えることで議論や意見を強める時に使う表現)

6. Giving Examples 例を挙げる

For example / For instance / In particular	例えば、
Let me give you some examples.	例を挙げます。
Let me explain further.	もう少し説明させて下さい。

7. Giving Reasons 理由を示す

The main reason is …	主な理由は
This is the reason why …	これが〜の理由です。
That is why …	だから〜なのです。

8. Citing Sources データの出典を示す

According to Webster's Dictionary,	ウェブスターの辞書によれば
A recent study by the University of Michigan suggests that …	ミシガン大学の最近の研究では〜のようなことを示しています。
The Labor Ministry data shows that …	厚生労働省のデータは〜のようなことを示しています。

9. Comparison & Contrast 比較と対照

On the other hand,	その反面、
However,	しかし、
My father likes fish while my mother likes meat.	父は魚が好きですが母は肉が好きです。

10. Repeating what you said 言及したことを繰り返す

As I said,	お話しましたように、
So far, I have explained …	ここまでご説明してきたことは
Up to here, I have talked about …	ここまでお話してきたことは

11. Paraphrasing 言及したことを言い換える

Let me put it this way.	次のように言い換えることができます。
In other words,	言い換えると、
Let me put it differently.	言い換えると次のようになります。
That is to say,	すなわち、つまり

12. Conclusion 結論

In short, / In conclusion, / In summary, / In brief,	まとめると、
I've talked about / I talked about (three points)	(3つのポイント)についてお話しました。
I'd like to insist that we should …	〜である、と主張します。
To sum up, / The point is	まとめますと、要約しますと
At the end of my speech,	スピーチの最後で、

13. Concluding remarks 結びの言葉

Thank you …	どうも有り難うございました。
Thank you for listening.	ご清聴、ありがとうございました。
Thank you for your attention.	ご清聴、ありがとうございました。
It was a great pleasure to speak to you today.	本日は皆さんにお話できて嬉しいです。
Thank you all for coming today.	ご来場ありがとうございました。

Useful Expressions for Responding

■ 受け答えをするときの英語表現集

1. Stating opinions 意見を述べる

In my opinion,	私の意見では、
My impression is …	私の印象では
From my point of view,	私の見方では、
As far as I'm concerned,	私の立場から申し上げますと、
I think / I don't think that …	～だと思います/ではないと思います。
All I can say is,	つまり私の申し上げられることは、
My opinion is …	私の意見は～です。
I believe that …	私は～だと信じます。

2. Asking for opinions

What do you think about …?	～についてどう思いますか。
What is your opinion about …?	～についてあなたの意見はいかがですか。
How do you feel about …?	～についてどう感じますか。
What is your impression of …?	～についての印象はいかがですか。

3. Agreeing 賛成する

Yes, that's right/true.	そうですね。
You're right.	そうですね。
I agree with you	賛成します。
I'm in favor of … / I'm for …	～に賛成です。
I couldn't agree more.	大賛成です。
Same here.	同じ意見です。
That's a good idea.	よい考えですね。
Absolutely! / Definitely!	そのとおりです！
You can say that again!	おっしゃるとおりです！

I'm with her.	彼女に賛成です。
I think you made a good point.	おっしゃるとおりだと思います。
Yes, I understand.	そうですね、わかります。
Yes, you could be right.	おっしゃるとおりかもしれませんね。
That's a good point.	よい視点ですね、そのとおりです。
That's exactly what I think.	私もまったく同じ意見です。
I have no objection.	反対はしません。
I'm not opposed to …	〜に反対はしていません。
I'm convinced by …	〜に納得です。
I think so, too.	私もそう思います。

4. Disagreeing 反対

I don't think it's right.	そうでしょうか？
I don't think so.	そうだとは思われませんが。
My idea is kind of different.	私の意見は少し違います。
I'm opposed to … / I oppose … / I'm against …	〜には反対です。
I'm not convinced by …	〜には納得できません。
I don't see the value of …	〜する価値がわかりません。
… is not really convincing.	あまり納得いきません。
I don't agree.	賛成しかねます。

5. Softeners 言葉を和らげる

I hate to disagree with you, but …	お言葉ですが、
I accept your point of view, but …	あなたの見方には同意しますが、
I understand what you're saying, but …	おっしゃることはわかりますが、
Yes, that may be true, but I actually think …	そうかも知れません、でも
I understand your point, but …	あなたの言いたいことはわかりますが
You have a point, but …	いいところを突いていると思いますが

6. Asking for clarification 意味を確認する

I don't understand what you mean.	おっしゃる意味がよくわかりません。
I didn't catch the last part.	最後の部分がよくわかりませんでした。
I didn't get that.	そこがよくわかりませんでした。

Could you repeat that, please? / Could you explain that again?	もう一度お願いします。
Sorry, what did you say?	すみません、なんておっしゃいましたか。
What do you mean by …?	〜はどういう意味ですか。
Would you mind repeating that?	もう一度言っていただけますか。
Sorry?	なんとおっしゃいましたか。
I am not with you. /I'm not following you.	おっしゃることがわかりません。
What is the bar chart about?	この棒グラフは何について説明しているのですか。

Unit 1
About Myself

自己紹介を英語で書いて、プレゼンテーションをしてみましょう。

🎧 Listening 1

Let's get to know each other. Listen to the dialogue between new students at a welcome party in a cafeteria and answer the questions.

🔊 Track 1

1. Where is Yuta from? Where is Naomi from?

___

2. Where was Naomi born? Where was she brought up?

___

3. Why did Naomi choose this university?

___

4. Why did Yuta choose this university?

_____

5. What does Yuta study at university?

_____

Work in pairs.

A: Hello. I'm _____. Nice to meet you.

B: I'm _____. Nice to meet you, too.

A: Where are you from? I'm from _____.

B: I'm from _____. Why did you come to this university?

A: _____. And, you? Why did you choose this university?

B: _____.

Speaking

A. Work in a pair. First, form questions. Then, ask the questions to your partner.

Questions   **Target answers**

1. _____   My name is Ken.

   Your partner: _____

2. _____   I'm from Hokkaido.

   Your partner: _____

3. _____   I went to Minato High School.

   Your partner: _____

4. _____   I live in Kawasaki.

   Your partner: _____

5. _____   I study law.

   Your partner: _____

6. _____   I listen to music and watch movies in my free time.

   Your partner: _____

B. Make a group of four with the pair next to you. Introduce your partner to the group.

(Example) Hi, I would like to introduce my partner to you. His/Her name is …….

 Writing

A. Study Eri's profile. Ask and answer the questions below with your partner.

My Profile
Name: Eri Nakano
Date of Birth: November 13, 2000
Place of Birth: Chiba
Nationality: Japanese
Education: graduated from Shueikan High School on March 31st, 2018
Working Experience:
worked as a cashier at a convenience store during the summer of 2016
worked as a volunteer at a charity concert in February 2018
Qualifications: driving license, scored 500 on TOEIC (November, 2017)
Favorite Things to Do: dancing, singing, listening to music

1. Where was Eri born?

   _____

2. Which high school did she graduate from?

   _____

3. What score did she get on the TOEIC test?

   _____

4. What jobs did she do part time?

   _____

   _____

5. What does she enjoy?

   _____

B. Write your own profile.

My Profile

Name:
Date of Birth:
Place of Birth:
Nationality:
Education:
Working Experience:

Qualifications:
Favorite Things to Do:

Listening 2

Listen to Eri's speech, and fill in the blanks.

Track 2

My Name is Eri Nakano. I was born in Chiba in (1.   ). My family (2.   ) to Osaka when I was ten. I (3.   ) Shueikan High School and entered Metropolitan University. I'm (4.   ) in computer science. I have a lot of work to do and sometimes I have to stay late at university to do assignments and learn computer programming.

I love music and enjoy singing and (5.   ). I started dancing when I was three. My mother just (6.   ) me to a local ballet school, and I loved it. When I was at junior high school, I (7.   ) going to dance lessons. I hated the strict teachers, frilly (8.   ) and everything. When I was a high school student, I started to dance again, not classical dancing but hip-hop and (9.   ) dancing. I am really happy when I am dancing. On weekends, my friends and I get (10.   ) and dance sometimes in hired studios and other times at local (11.   ). Now we are practicing for the summer festival. I hope I will see some of (12.   ) there.

Prepare your speech

Write about yourself.

In the 1st paragraph, write about your background.

In the 2nd paragraph, write about one of the following:

1. what you enjoy or what you regularly do
   - When did you start to do it?
   - How long have you been doing it?
   - How often do you do it?
   - Why do you like to do it?
   - Do you have any future plans about the activity?

2. what you are interested in doing, studying or learning
   - Why are you interested in it?
   - What would you like to do with it?
   - How can you do it? Do you need anything or any help to achieve your goal?

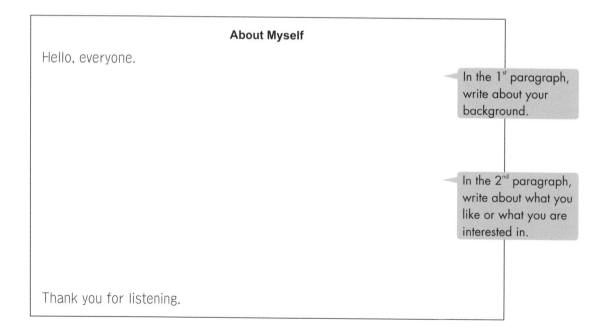

Peer Editing

Exchange your drafts and correct errors if any. Make comments to improve your partner's speech.

Unit 2

My Hero

あなたにとってのヒーローは誰ですか。歴史上の人物または身近な人など、あなたが尊敬する、大好きな人物について話してみましょう。

Getting ready

A. When you hear the word " hero", who do you think of?

_____

B. How do you describe your hero? What words would you like to use? Put down some nouns and adjectives which describe your hero. First, write them in Japanese and then try to put them into English. You can use your dictionary.

日本語		English	日本語		English
スポーツ選手	→	athlete	すごい技術	→	fantastic skill
●	→		●	→	
●	→		●	→	
●	→		●	→	
●	→		●	→	

Listening 1

A. Match English expressions with Japanese.

1. for the first time (　　)
2. fascinated (　　)
3. outstanding (　　)
4. apparent (　　)
5. distinguished (　　)

ア　準優勝
イ　有名な
ウ　病気にかかる
エ　明らかな
オ　前途有望な

6. treatment (　　)　　　　　　　　カ　わくわくさせる

7. runner-up (　　)　　　　　　　　キ　治療

8. thrill (　　)　　　　　　　　　　ク　飛び抜けている

9. suffer from (　　)　　　　　　　ケ　魅了される

10. promising (　　)　　　　　　　コ　初めて

B. Listen and fill in the blanks.

Track 3

Hello, my name is Hiroshi. Today, I'd like to talk about a person I admire, my hero.

My hero is Lionel Messi, a soccer player. I saw him (1.　　　　　　) when I was a sixth grader in elementary school. He was on TV, playing as a member of the Argentinian national team in the 2010 World Cup which was held in South Africa. I was (2.　　　　　　) his beautiful dribbling and passion for scoring goals. I knew his performance was outstanding because I had been playing soccer since I was ten.

Lionel Messi was born on (3.　　　　　　) in Rosario, Argentina to a working class family. He began playing soccer in local clubs (4.　　　　　　) because his brothers played soccer and his father was a coach. Soon his talent was apparent and his future as a professional player (5.　　　　　　).

However, at the age of 11, he was discovered to be suffering from a growth hormone deficiency, which would force him to give up his career. Then (6.　　　　　　) a trial with FC Barcelona, a distinguished Spanish club and fortunately the club offered him a contract which included paying for his treatment. Messi moved to Barcelona with his family and completed the treatment thanks to the club's support.

Messi (7.　　　　　　) in the Spanish league in 2004. Since then, he has been playing as a leading member of Barcelona and one of the most recognized athletes of the world. He has won the FIFA Ballon d'Or award (the World's Best Player of the Year Award) five times and led Argentina to winning the Gold Medal at the 2008 Olympic Games and to being the runner-up in the 2014 World Cup.

Being a splendid player, he is also known for his (8.　　　　　　) helping disadvantaged children. He has served as a UNICEF

Goodwill Ambassador and founded his own organization, which supports children's health care, education, and soccer clubs.

Lionel Messi is my hero because he thrills us both on and off the pitch.

🎧 Listening 2

A. Match English expressions with Japanese.

1. architect ( )
2. courageous ( )
3. in need of ~ ( )
4. kidney ( )
5. donate ( )
6. office clerk ( )
7. hardship ( )
8. tremendous effort ( )

ア 勇気のある
イ すごい努力
ウ 事務員
エ 苦境
オ 提供する
カ 建築家
キ 腎臓
ク ～を必要とする

B. Listen to the following speech and try to catch the actual sounds of the speaker. Then listen again and read aloud along with the speaker.

🔊 Track 4

My uncle Takeo is such a loving person. He is my father's younger brother. He was born on March 15, 1970. He is an architect who works hard every day to support his family.

Uncle Takeo is my hero because he is very courageous. Five years ago, my father became ill and the only way to survive was to get a kidney transplant. Uncle Takeo volunteered to donate his kidney to my father. His courage and love saved my father's life.

He is a man of will and patience. When he was a boy, his family was very poor and he couldn't receive a college education. He worked full time as an office clerk while studying by himself. After several years of tremendous effort, he finally became a qualified architect and made his dream come true.

He is hard working and caring. He never fails to complete any tasks he sets out to do. He always gives us help when we need it. He has let me know that I can succeed in anything I put my mind to, and gives me hope for a better future. Although he is not famous or rich, I think he is great. He is absolutely my hero.

C. Read the speech above again and write T for the statements which match the speech and write F for the ones which don't match the speech.

(　) Takeo is the speaker's brother.
(　) Five years ago, the speaker's father was in need of a new kidney.
(　) Takeo is from a very rich family.
(　) Takeo became an architect without going to university.
(　) The speaker thinks Takeo is a hero because he is courageous and hardworking.

D. Answer the following questions.

1. Who is the speaker's hero?
_____

2. Describe the relation between the hero and the speaker.
_____

3. What makes him the speaker's hero?
_____
_____

4. How has he influenced the speaker's life?
_____
_____

Listening 3

A. Match English expressions with Japanese.

1. resistance (　)　　　　ア　嫌がらせ
2. discrimination (　)　　イ　記述
3. civil rights (　)　　　　ウ　差別
4. influence (　)　　　　　エ　影響を与える
5. description (　)　　　　オ　抵抗
6. independence (　)　　　カ　捧げる
7. harassment (　)　　　　キ　独立
8. dedicate (　)　　　　　ク　公民権

B. Listen and fill in the blanks.

🔊 Track 5

My hero is Mahatma Gandhi, a political leader of India. I knew him (1. _____) in the social study class when I was a junior high school student. The textbook showed only a (2. _____) about him and a photo of a thin, plainly dressed old man with a gentle gaze. Soon after that, I had a chance to watch a movie about his life and learned he was such a great person.

His real name is Mohandas Karamchand Gandhi. He was born on (3. _____) at Porbandar, in the present-day Indian state of Gujarat. His father was the chief minister of the county, but his family was not rich. He was a shy boy. (4. _____), Gandhi left home to study law in London. After graduation, he started to work as a lawyer in South Africa where he spent the next 20 years.

As an Indian immigrant, Gandhi experienced (5. _____). For example, he was not allowed to sit with European passengers in the stagecoach and told to sit on the floor near the driver, and beaten up when he refused. That kind of experience made him decide to be a (6. _____). He started to fight for his fellow Indian residents but his way of fighting was not through force or violence but a way called "passive resistance".

He returned to India in 1915. At that time, India was under the colonial rule of the British and again he saw Indian people being forced to live in an (7. _____). Despite harassment and repeated arrests by the authorities, he continued to carry out civil disobedience campaigns against the colonial government and the Indians (8. _____) in 1947. Unfortunately, the country was divided into two, India and Pakistan, because of their different religions. Gandhi was shot by a Hindu fanatic who was angry about the separation of the country and died at the age of 78 in 1948.

He (9. _____) to his fellow citizens and showed them that they could make a change by fighting with "non-violence". His idea influenced many politicians and artists including Martin Luther King Jr. and John Lennon. He is definitely (10. _____) political leaders of the 20th century and he makes me think about civil rights and society. There is still so much we can learn from him.

C. Read the speech above again and answer the questions.

1. How did the speaker come to learn about Gandhi?

2. When and where was Gandhi born?

3. Where did he start his first job?

4. What made him decide to be a civil rights activist?

5. What did he do after he returned his home country?

6. What was unique about his way of fighting injustice?

Research

Answer the questions about your hero, following the example of Hiroshi from *Listening 1*. You may need to make research with books or on the Internet to find the answers. If your hero is somebody close to you, you can interview him/her in person.

1. Who is your hero?

   Hiroshi's answer (以下H): My hero is Lionel Messi.

2. What is his/her profession?

   H: He is a soccer player.

3. How and when did you learn about him/her for the first time? How did you feel then?

   H: I saw him on TV when I was a sixth grader. He was playing at 2010 World Cup. I was fascinated by his beautiful dribbling and his passion.

4. When and where was he/she born?

   H: He was born on 24 June 1987, in Rosario, Argentina.

5. What kind of childhood did he/she have?

   H: He is a son of a working-class family. He began playing soccer from an early age.

6. When and how did he/she start his/her career?

   H: He started to play in a local team. As a pro, he signed the contract with FC Barcelona at the age of 13.

7. What kind of hardship did he/she go through? How did he/she overcome the hardship?

   H: At age of 11, he was diagnosed with growth hormone deficiency but he was offered a contract by FC Barcelona which was willing to pay for his treatment.

8. What is his/her greatest achievement?

   H: He has won FIFA Ballon d'Or award five times and led Argentina to the Gold Medal in the 2008 Olympic Games and to being the runner-up in the 2014 World Cup.

9. What is he/she doing now?

   H: He is still playing as a member of FC Barcelona.

10. What makes him/her your hero?

    H: He thrills us both on and off the pitch.

💬 Speaking

Ask your partner about his/her hero using the questions in the previous section.

📝 Prepare your speech

Now write your own speech using the sample expressions and your answers in *Research* section.

☞ **Key Point!**

- Describe your hero and your relation to him/her. How did you know him/her?
- Explain why he/she is your hero.
- Share how your hero has influenced your life, decisions, career path, etc.

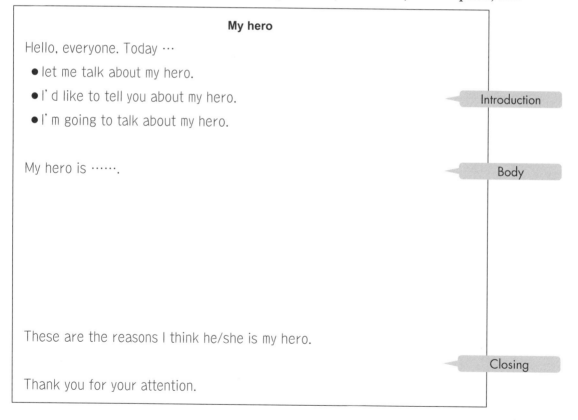

🔍 Peer Editing

Exchange your drafts and correct errors if any. Make comments to improve your partner's speech.

Unit 3

Describing Pictures and Photos

ここでは、写真の情景を具体的に説明したり、物の位置関係を説明したりする練習をしましょう。

Getting ready

Complete the sentences with the appropriate present progressive (continuous) form to say what the people in the pictures are doing. Use the verbs in the box.

| sweep | queue | consult | dance | shop for | climb |

1. Two people (   ) a lawyer about their tax.

2. The children (   ) to piano music.

3. Two pupils (　　　　) the floor.

4. A man wearing a helmet (　　　　) a step.

5. Many people (　　　　) on the street.

6. A woman (　　　　　　　) groceries.

Listening 1

Vocabulary preview

Put into Japanese.

1. in the foreground _____
2. in the background _____
3. in the upper part _____
4. in the lower part _____
5. in the left-upper part _____
6. in the right-upper part _____
7. in the central part _____
8. in front of ~ _____
9. behind _____
10. beside _____
11. next to _____
12. along _____
13. down below _____
14. side by side _____
15. in a row _____
16. across from _____
17. on the right _____
18. on the left _____

Describing Pictures and Photos

You will hear the two statements for each picture. Listen and fill in the blanks. Then choose the one statement that best describes the picture.

Track 6

1.

    a. Four dresses are arranged on display (　　　　).
    b. Four coats are hanging on display (　　　　).

2.

    a. The boy (　　　　) is holding a map (　　　　).
    b. The girl (　　　　) is holding a map (　　　　).

3.

   a. The female nurse is standing (　　　　　).
   b. The male nurse is standing (　　　　　).

4.

   a. The man (　　　　　) is crossing his legs and entertaining the woman.
   b. The woman is sitting (　　　　　) the sofa and being entertained by four men.

Describing Pictures and Photos

Exercise

A. Write one sentence based on the each photo below. Use the helping words and phrases given. You may change the forms of the words and use them in any order.

1. (cabin crew / walk smartly)

2. (plane / step off)

33

Unit 3

3. (woman / reception desk)

4. (passengers / two-story train)

B. Bring your own photo. Write two words or phrases on the back of the photo. Exchange your photos with your classmates. Make one sentence based on the photo by using those key words.

1. _____
2. _____
3. _____

🎧 Listening 2

Listen and fill in the blanks.

This is a picture of three people who are sitting (1. _____) on the rock. (2. _____) of the picture, we cannot see their faces but only their feet and legs. Perhaps it is a holiday season, and they (3. _____) a wonderful view and people (4. _____). Three of them (5. _____) trousers and sneakers. (6. _____), from left to right, you can see cars parked (7. _____). There seem to be quite a lot of people visiting this area. It must be a popular tourist spot, like a national wild-life park. (8. _____), there is an open field with desert trees.

Unit 3

📝 Prepare your speech

A. Find your own interesting photo and explain it.

☞ **Key point!**
- 写真の概要を述べる
- 人や物の位置関係を示す
- 人が複数いる場合、共通点を述べる
- 動作について述べる
- 服装について述べる
- 写真をよく見て、まだ描写していないことを探したり、写真について自分の意見や推測を述べたりしてみましょう。

B. Write your paragraph.

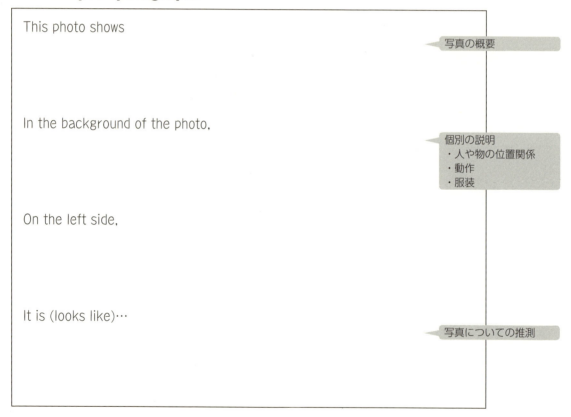

This photo shows

In the background of the photo,

On the left side,

It is (looks like)…

🔍 Peer Editing

Exchange your drafts and correct errors if any. Make comments to improve your partner's speech.

Unit 4

Giving Instructions

やり方や手順の説明を、聴衆に向かって説明する練習をしましょう。パワーポイントを使うと、よりわかりやすく具体的な説明ができます。

Getting ready

A. Match the pictures with the expressions in the list below.

1.   2.   3.   4.

(　　)　　(　　)　　(　　)　　(　　)

5.   6.   7.   8.

(　　)　　(　　)　　(　　)　　(　　)

```
stir   chop   cut   fry   boil   beat   slice   peel
```

B. Put into English.

1. 材料をなべに入れる _____
2. 塩、コショウする _____
3. 20分煮る _____
4. 野菜をいためる _____

Exercise 1

The following sentences are instructions for a recipe, but in the wrong order. Put the sentences into the right order. What recipe are they for?

1. Add some canned tomatoes, stir and cook for 15 to 20 minutes.
2. Add a stock cube, and season with some salt and pepper.
3. Add some minced meat and fry further.
4. Cook five more minutes until the sauce is creamy.
5. Chop an onion and fry it.

Correct order: ___ → ___ → ___ → ___ → ___

This is a recipe for (   ).

Exercise 2

A. Fill in the blanks of the instructions for preparing cup noodles.

First, (1.   ) water.

(2.   ), open the seal of the cup. Take out the bags of soup powder and put the contents in the cup.

After that, (3.   ) the hot water into the cup.

And then, close the seal and (4.   ) three minutes.

Finally, remove the seal, (5.   ) them well. Now they are ready to eat.

B. Go back to the recipe of *Exercise 1*. Rewrite the recipe with connectors such as 'first' and 'then'.

First, _____

Then, _____

After that _____

And then _____

Finally _____

Giving Instructions

🎧 Listening

Listen and fill in the blanks.

🔊 Track 8

Brian arrived in Japan a few hours ago. He is staying with Taro's family. Taro is showing him how to take a bath.

I'm going to (1. _____) how to take a Japanese bath. You need a face towel to (2. _____) a Japanese bath. You might take a shower in the morning in your country, but we usually take a bath in the evening. First, (3. _____) the cover of the bathtub. Then, (4. _____) your body with a shower or hot water in the tub. And then, get in the bathtub and (5. _____) yourself. Next, wash your hair and body (6. _____) the bathtub. Use your towel for washing. Rinse your hair and body well (7. _____) the soap is all removed. After that, get in the bathtub again and (8. _____). (9. _____) you are finished, put the cover on the bathtub. Don't (10. _____) the water. Someone will use the bath water after you.

✍ Exercise 3

A. Make two sentences into one by using 'until'.

1. You bake it. Then, it is golden brown.
   _____

2. Beat the egg white. Then, it is stiff.
   _____

3. Toast the bread. Then the cheese (on the toast) melts.
   _____

B. Put Japanese into English by using 'when'.

1. 指示がスクリーンに出てきたら、press the correct buttons.
   _____

2. 煮えたら、cool it for ten minutes.
   _____

3. 家に入るときは、take off your shoes.
   _____

Exercise 4

Write instructions with your partner for:

making tea, fried eggs, instant noodles, pancake, ham sandwiches and cooking rice

Exercise 5

A. This is Tomoko's script for presentation. Which slide would she show as she speaks? Choose one for 1 to 8 from the choices a to h below.

Track 9

How to make coffee from dandelions

1. (a) Hello everyone. Today I'd like to show you how to make coffee from dandelions. (Dandelions are called tampopo in Japanese.) 2. (   ) First, you have to find well-grown dandelions and dig up their roots. They have very deep roots. So, you may have a hard time digging them. 3. (   ) Second, you have to wash these roots to remove dirt. 4. (   ) Next, cut these roots into 1-centimeter pieces, and soak them in water for three hours. This is to remove the bitterness. 5. (   ) This process is very important. If you skip this, you won't be able to drink your coffee because it'll be too bitter. 6. (   ) After this process, dry them in the sun for three days and roast them as you roast coffee beans. 7. (   ) Finally, you have to crush them into powder by using a coffee mill or a food processor and extract the essence. 8. (   ) Dandelion coffee tastes bitter like coffee but contains a high level of polyphenols and has no caffeine. So, it's good for pregnant women, children, and elderly people.

a. How to make coffee from dandelions.

b. … Bitter!!!!

c. Step (   ): _____

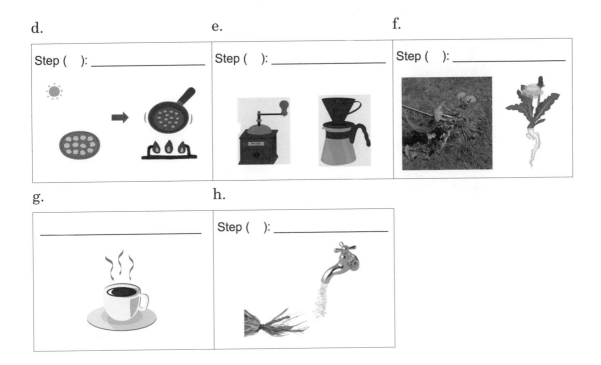

B. Look at the slides once again.

1. What title would you give to each of the slides c to h? Choose one from the choices below.

   Dry and roast.   Enjoy dandelion coffee!   Wash roots.   Dig up roots.
   Cut roots and soak in water.   Crush and extract.

   c. _____   d. _____
   e. _____   f. _____
   g. _____   h. _____

2. Put a number to each step from 1 to 5.
   c. Step (   )   d. Step (   )   e. Step (   )   f. Step (   )   h. Step (   )

📝 Prepare your speech

List of possible topics

1. Recipes: you can show how to cook your favorite dish.

2. You can show how to use or play something.
   • how to play sports, games, musical instruments, etc
   • You can demonstrate by showing the instrument you play (with).

3. Japanese customs, cultures or rules which people from different cultures might not be familiar with
- how to buy a train pass
- how to prepare a bento-box
- how to eat sushi
- how to enjoy cherry blossom viewing

4. You can show how to get to your house from your university.

5. You can show your favorite way to relax, sleep well, etc.
- how to relax
- how to boost your energy
- how to refresh yourself

6. You can give instructions on household chores or gardening.
- how to take out the trash
- how to plant tulips
- how to grow basil
- how to grow potatoes

7. You can show how to use tools, machines, and computers etc.
- how to transfer pictures from a digital camera onto your computer
- how to make PowerPoint slides

8. You can explain procedures for conducting an experiment or test in your field of study.
- how to use a stereo-microscope
- how to test the quality of an egg
- how to observe the pigment of vegetables

> **Just a minute!**
>
> インターネットを見るとたくさん英語のレシピがあります。これをコピー&ペーストして、自分の原稿にしちゃおうかな、という誘惑にかられるかもしれません。でも、それは絶対にしてはいけません。
>
> 他人の書いたものを，出典を明らかにせずに写して使うことは、**Plagiarism** といって、学術界で最も重大な違反です。無断で借用した人の学力やモラルが疑われることに加えて、学位はく奪、退学などの厳罰が課せられることもあります。
>
> この unit の課題は、やり方や手順を、自分の英語で他の人に伝える、ということです。

Giving Instructions

6 steps to presentation

1. 【トピックの決定】First, decide your title.
2. 【手順の図式化】Second, draw a picture for each step. These pictures can be used for your PowerPoint slides.
3. 【手順の文章化】Third, write a simple instruction sentence for each step. Remember to use an imperative form (命令文).

Title: How to _____

Slides	Sentences for each step
	Step 1
	Step 2
	Step 3
	Step 4
	Step 5

4. 【必要なものまたは材料の確認】After making a basic outline, write down what is necessary for your instruction.
5. 【発表原稿の完成】Write up your draft by using cohesive devices (接続表現) such as "first", "second", and "until", "when".

A tip for better writing:

Add a sentence or two after outlining some steps to give further details or explain why this step is important.
→See 'How to make dandelion coffee' on p.40.
Line 4: They have very deep roots.
Lines 7 and 8: This is to remove the bitterness. This process is very important. If you skip this, you cannot drink your coffee because it is too bitter.

---

6. 【発表練習】Try READ and LOOK UP to practice your presentation!

Unit 5

Promoting Places or Products

このユニットでは商品や場所についての紹介を行うスピーチを作ってみましょう。聴衆によく伝わるよう、ポイントを明確に、わかりやすく、繰り返し述べることが大切です。

Getting ready

Answer the quizzes with your partner. Pay attention to the usage of adjectives (形容詞).

1. This is a Japanese city with a <u>long</u> history. There are many <u>historic</u> temples and shrines. It is also <u>famous</u> for its <u>formal</u> traditions such as <u>exquisite</u> kaiseki dining and <u>beautiful</u> apprentices of geisha.
   Answer: ＿＿＿＿＿＿＿＿＿＿

2. This is a <u>European</u> country with a <u>long</u> coastline. Its capital is especially <u>famous</u> for its <u>ancient</u> ruins and <u>religious</u> buildings. If you visit, you will enjoy <u>authentic</u> pizza and pasta.
   Answer: ＿＿＿＿＿＿＿＿＿＿

3. This product is a very <u>popular</u> smartphone accessory. You can take a photo of yourself. It comes in a lot of <u>different</u> sizes, but is commonly <u>long</u> and <u>compact</u>.
   Answer: ＿＿＿＿＿＿＿＿＿＿

4. This is a <u>low</u> <u>wooden</u> table used in the wintertime in Japan. The table has an <u>electric</u> heater inside and is covered by <u>heavy</u> blanket. It keeps you <u>warm</u> and <u>relaxed</u>.
   Answer: ＿＿＿＿＿＿＿＿＿＿

☞ **Make your own quiz and see if your partner can guess the answer.**

Listening 1

Listen to the conversation and fill in the blanks. Then answer the question.

🔊 Track 10

A: I'm trying to find a (1._____) to take my girlfriend on her birthday. Do you know any good places in the city?

B: Oh, I know one. There is a great Italian restaurant on Beach Street. They serve very (2._____) Italian home style dishes. It's right on the pier, so it has a (3._____).

A: Sounds great. My girlfriend loves Italian food. What's the name of the restaurant?

B: Antonio's. Their prices are very (4._____) and the service is (5._____), too. They have a special birthday service for you if you dine on your birthday.

A: Wow. That's perfect. Her birthday is this Sunday. I will take her there then.

B: I recommend you (6._____) in advance. It is such a popular place and there is always a long waiting line on weekends.

A: Ok, I will do that right away. Do you know the telephone number?

B: No. but you can find their website and make a reservation through the Internet.

What are some of the selling points of this restaurant? List at least three points.

_____
_____
_____
_____

Exercise

A. What adjectives do you use for describing things or places? Choose a word for each blank from the list below.

1. 役立つ機能 _____ function
2. 便利な道具 _____ tool
3. 値段の高くない家具 _____ furniture
4. おいしいステーキ _____ steak
5. 魅力的な内装 _____ interior
6. 伝統的な祭り _____ festival
7. 歴史ある建物 _____ building
8. 華麗なドレス _____ dress
9. 興味深い慣習 _____ custom
10. さわやかな飲み物 _____ drink
11. 珍しい動物 _____ animal
12. 印象的な映画 _____ movie
13. リラックスできる椅子 _____ chair
14. 快適な空間 _____ space

| traditional | inexpensive | interesting | gorgeous | tasty | comfortable | relaxing | historic |
| convenient | refreshing | attractive | rare | impressive | useful |

B. Describe your favorite place; your hometown or any place you visit often.

1. Place of your choice: _____
2. List adjectives you will use to describe the place. (e.g: quiet, relaxing, charming)
   _____
3. Now, write 3 sentences to describe the place using the adjectives you listed above.
   _____
   _____
   _____
4. Then, make pairs and tell your partner about your favorite place.

Listening 2

Listen to the speech and answer the questions.

Track 11

1. How do you get to Takayama?
   _____
   _____

2. What attractions or sight-seeing spots are there in Takayama?
   _____
   _____

3. What is the Takayama Festival like?

Speech script

以下の原稿を参考にしてスピーチのフォーマットを学習しましょう。**First, second, next** などを用いて繰り返しているところに注意しながら読みましょう。

My Hometown, Takayama (242 words)

[Introduction]

Good morning, everyone. Have you ever visited Takayama? Today, I would like to tell you about my hometown of Takayama. First, I'm going to tell you where it is, and second, I'm going to tell you its attractions.

これから述べることを伝える

[Body 1]

First, Takayama is in Gifu prefecture. The fastest way to get to Takayama from Tokyo or Osaka is to use the Shinkansen to Nagoya, and then use the JR line to Takayama. It takes about 4 hours either from Tokyo or Osaka.

[Body 2]

Next, I'll tell you about its attractions. Takayama is an old castle town surrounded by beautiful mountains. It has well-preserved old streets with old houses from the Edo period. Lively morning markets which originated in the Edo period are also famous and attract many tourists. Takayama is well-known for the Takayama festival which is held twice a year in spring and fall. It is a unique festival with a parade of various colorful floats. It is probably one of the most beautiful festivals in Japan. The popular but exclusive regional food is Hida beef, which is very tender and delicious. For more casual dining, you can enjoy our famous local ramen, called Takayama ramen.

[Conclusion]

Today, I told you about my hometown; its location and its attractions. Please remember that Takayama is only 4 hours away from Tokyo or Osaka and it is an attractive city with a Japanese traditional atmosphere and gourmet food. I hope you'll visit Takayama in the near future.

強調したいことを繰り返す

Prepare your speech

Think of something or some place you want to recommend to other people and prepare your speech.

A thing/place you recommend to other people: _____

☞ **Key point!**

Use adjectives (形容詞) effectively to describe the thing/ place so that listeners can get the clear image of what you are talking about.

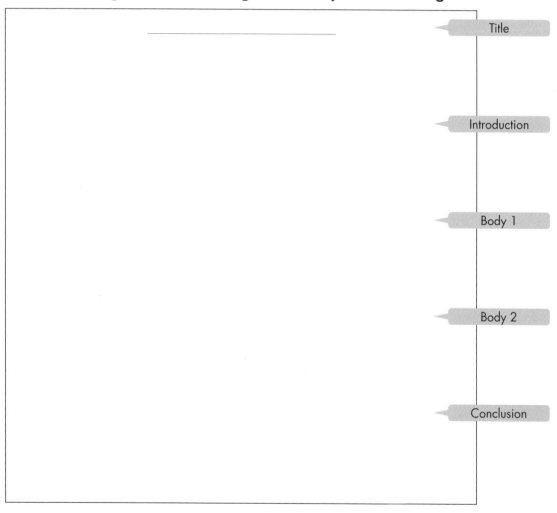

Peer Editing

Exchange your drafts and correct errors if any. Make comments to improve your partner's speech.

Unit 6

Causes and Effects

物事の原因や、その影響について述べましょう。Part I では causes と effects を確認、Part II では causes, Part III では effects を論じます。

Part I

Cause and effect

Getting ready

Describe what happens in each picture in the past tense. Then, practice two types of conversation with your partner.

Example

a.

b.

_____   _____

(1) Talking about the effect

A: The woman lost her house keys.

B: What was the effect?

A: She couldn't get into her house.

B: The woman lost her house keys. <u>As a result</u>, she couldn't get into her house.

49

(2) Talking about the cause

A: The woman couldn't get into her house.

B: Why couldn't she get into her house?

A: Because she lost her house keys.

B: The woman couldn't get into her house <u>because</u> she lost her house keys.

1. a.

b.

(1) Talking about the effect

A: _____

B: What was the effect?

A: _____

B: _____

(2) Talking about the cause

A: _____

B: Why did you have them?

A: _____

B: _____

Causes and Effects

2. a. _____ b. _____

(1) Talking about the effect

A: _____
B: _____
A: _____
B: _____

(2) Talking about the cause

A: _____
B: _____
A: _____
B: _____

👆 Exercise 1

Choose the best expression for each blank from the list on the next page.

1. Cause: a typhoon

   Effects: a. _____

   b. schools being closed

   c. floods and mudslides

2. Cause: _____

   Effects: a. saving money (because less expensive than eating out)

   b. _____

   c. washing up needed

51

3. Cause: my new job
   Effects: a. _____
       b. more money
       c. happier than before

4. Cause: _____
   Effects: a. turning on the air conditioner
       b. _____
       c. very few people walking during the day

| cooking at home   more responsibility   trains and flights delayed or cancelled
| eating a lot of ice cream   more nutritious and well-balanced meals   a high temperature |

Exercise 2

Does each paragraph discuss causes or effects? Fill in the blanks.

1. This paragraph is about (causes / effects).

The typhoon (   ) us very badly. For one thing, it brought heavy rain and strong winds, and a lot of trains were delayed, all flights cancelled. In addition, schools were closed and students had to stay at home. Finally, the heavy rain resulted in flooding and mudslides.

2. This paragraph is about (causes / effects).

There are several reasons (   ) I left my former job. First of all, I was not happy with my job. It was boring and I couldn't learn anything new. Besides, the salary was low and it was hard to make ends meet. Working hours were long, and they gave me few paid holidays. I'm glad I changed my job.

Part II
Focus on causes

Listening 1

Mina and Takashi are talking about reading newspapers. Do they read newspapers? Why or why not?

First listening
Fill in the blanks.

🔊 Track 12

Mina (　　　　) newspapers while Takashi (　　　　).

Second listening
Write down the words and phrases you hear.

🔊 Track 12

Mina:

Takashi:

Work in pairs. Write sentences which explain their reasons.

Mina (　　　　) newspapers because
1. _____
2. _____
3. _____
4. _____

Takashi (　　　　) newspapers because
1. _____
2. _____
3. _____

Exercise 3

Why do you shop online? Give reasons.

1. It is (　　　　　). You don't have to visit shops and you can save time.
2. It is (　　　). Your product is delivered to your home the next day of your order.
3. You can compare prices on websites and choose the (　　　) prices.
4. You can get products which were not available (　　　) online shopping was common.
5. If you have changed your mind, you can (　　　) your order.

53

Unit 6

Writing 1

Write a passage about why people shop online.

Writing 2

Are there any products/things you prefer to buy from shops rather than online? Why? Give reasons in a few sentences.

Part III
Focus on effects

🎧 Listening 2

First listening

What is the topic of the talk? Answer in four words.

🔊 Track 13

_____ _____ ____ _____

Second listening

Work in pairs and complete the outline of the talk.

🔊 Track 13

The main idea: _____

Effect 1: _____
Effect 2: _____
Effect 3: _____
_____

Read the script. What example is given to each effect?

Example of effect 1: _____
_____
Example of effect 2: _____
Example of effect 3: _____

✏️ Writing 3

A. You are taking a yoga class. Write down the good effects yoga has on your life.

The main idea: Participating in yoga lessons has _____
_____
Effect 1: _____
Effect 2: _____
Effect 3: _____

B. Complete the passage by describing effects and giving examples.

I started to _____. This practice has had many positive effects on my life. Firstly, _____
_____
_____. Secondly, _____
_____
_____. Finally, _____.

Discussion

What good effects does a part-time job have on your life? Are there any bad effects?

Good effects
1. _____
2. _____
3. _____

Bad effects
1. _____
2. _____
3. _____

Prepare your speech

Write about what you do regularly or what you have just started to do. How has this habit/new thing affected your life?

List of possible topics
- keeping a dog
- using an iPhone
- working part-time
- getting up at 6:00
- reading a newspaper every day

Causes and Effects

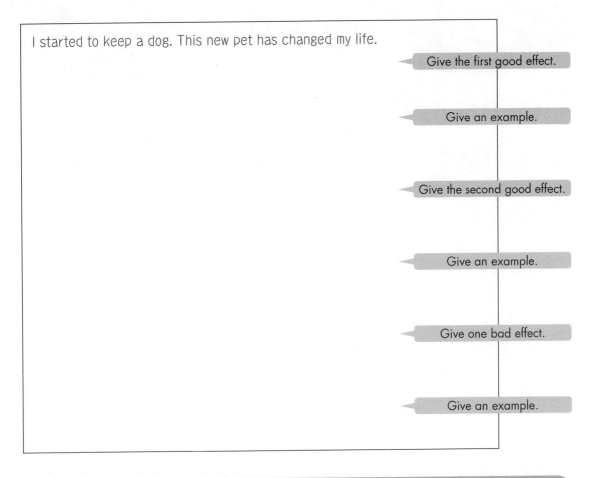

Peer Editing

Exchange your drafts and correct errors if any. Make comments to improve your partner's speech.

Unit 7

Comparing Two Things

2つのものを比較し、共通点や相違点を述べる練習をしましょう。

💡 Getting ready

A. Compare dogs and cats and complete the table.

Differences

	dogs	cats
size		
food		
habits		
character		
tricks		

B. Are there any similarities between dogs and cats?

Similarities

58

Reading

Read the passage and do the tasks below.

Track 14

  Dogs and cats are both popular pets. They share some similarities but they are (1.) in many ways. They are both mammals. A female dog or cat feeds her young with her milk. They both give birth to two or more puppies or kittens in one pregnancy. Both dogs and cats (2.) about 15 to 18 years if you take good care of them. Both dogs and cats make (3.): dogs bark and cats meow.

  Dogs and cats have differences, too. First of all, dogs vary in size while cats are about the same in (4.). They like different food. Dogs like meat, while cats like (5.). Their habits are different, too. You have to take a dog for a walk every day. On the other hand, you cannot (6.) cats. Dogs and cats have different (7.): dogs are obedient and loyal to their owners while cats are independent and self-reliant. You can teach some tricks to dogs. Not only 'wait' and 'go': some dogs can learn how to catch a ball or a Frisbee. But cats rarely learn (8.). It is very hard to teach cats 'give me a paw'. If you live with a dog and a cat, you will see the contrasts between them clearly.

1. Fill in the blanks.
2. Underline the expressions which signal likenesses or differences.
3. Choose sentences which give examples of the preceding general statements.
 （一般的なことを述べた文に続いて、それに対する具体的な例を挙げている文を選びなさい。）

General statements	Examples
They are both mammals.	A female dog or cat feeds her young with her milk.

Unit 7

Structure of the paragraphs

Fill in the blanks.

1st paragraph

　The (　　　　　　　) of dogs and cats are described.

2nd paragraph

　The (　　　　　　　) of dogs and cats are described.

Exercise 1

Look at the table and fill in the blanks of the passage below.

	Italiana	The Ladybird Cafe
meals I had	lunch	dinner
food	delicious	terrible
atmosphere	bright, clean, quiet	dark, dirty, noisy
waiters	more polite	rude
prices	reasonable	high

Comparisons between the two restaurants: Italiana and Ladybird Cafe

Track 15

　　When I was in Shinjuku last week, I ate at two very different restaurants. I had lunch at Italiana and (1.　　　　) at the Ladybird Cafe. First of all, the food at Italiana was (2.　　　　　), but the food at the Ladybird Cafe was (3.　　　　). The atmosphere at Italiana was much (4.　　　　) than the one at the Ladybird Cafe. Italiana was bright, (5.　　　　) and quiet. (6.　　　　　), the Ladybird Cafe was dark, dirty and noisy. The waiters at Italiana were much more (7.　　　) than the (8.　　　) at the Ladybird Cafe. In fact, the waiters at Ladybird Cafe were quite (9.　　　　). Finally, the prices at Italiana were reasonable while the prices at the Ladybird Cafe were high. A cup of coffee was 300 yen at Italiana whereas it was 500 yen at the Ladybird Cafe. Next time, I will go to (10.　　　　) for dinner.

Comparing Two Things

🎧 Listening

First listening

Listen to the conversation and draw a collar for each of the shirts below.

🔊 Track 16

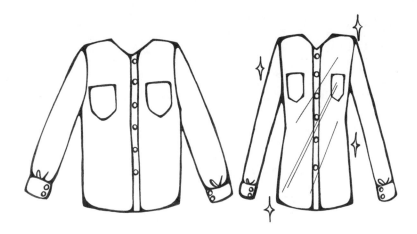

Second listening

Listen to the conversation once again and answer the questions.

🔊 Track 16

1. What are the similarities and differences of the two shirts? Fill in the table.

	The left shirt	**The right shirt**
similarities	Both shirts are	
differences		

2. What is John's problem?

He can't decide on one of the two shirts because _____

_____

_____

Exercise 2

Look at the table and write a paragraph about the sisters' differences.

	Sue	Linda
age	23	18
height	172 cm	155 cm
eye color	blue	brown
hair color	blond	dark
personality	serious, quiet	outgoing, creative

Comparisons between two sisters: Sue and Linda

Sue and Linda are sisters, but they are different in many ways.

Writing 1

Compare a car (sedan) and a motorbike (250 cc) and write paragraphs.

Similarities

- You need a (　　　) to drive them.
- Both cars and motorbikes go on the (　　) side of the road.
- Both cars and motorbikes need (　　　) to run.
- Both cars and motorbikes can (　　　) more than one person.

Differences

appearance
• A car has four (　　　), while a motorbike has two.
• A car has a roof, but a motorbike doesn't.
passenger capacity
• A car can (　　　) four or five people, but a motorbike can (　　　) only two.

amount of fuel they use
• A car (　　　　) more gasoline than a motorbike.
protection
• You fasten a seatbelt when you drive, while you put on a (　　　　) when you ride on a motorbike.
others

Paragraphs

✏ Writing 2

Compare a bed and a futon and write paragraphs.

Similarities

Differences

occupancy

soft or hard to lie on

safety

dustiness

Paragraphs

📝 Prepare your speech

List of possible topics

1. entertainment
   - mobile phone game applications: (　　　　　) and (　　　　　)
   - Doraemon and Pikachu

2. music
   - music you used to listen to when you were in junior high school and music you are now listening to
   - your favorite karaoke song and your best friend's favorite song

3. sports
   - badminton and tennis
   - skiing and snowboarding
   - futsal and soccer

4. education
   - university and high school education
   - co-educational and single-sex education

5. food
   - two fast food restaurants
   - okonomiyaki and pizza

6. part-time jobs
   - a cashier at a convenience store and a waiter in a restaurant
   - a private tutor and a classroom teacher

7. others
- supermarkets and convenience stores
- Tokyo and your hometown
- a zoo and an aquarium

A. First, find some similarities between the two things which you are going to compare. Then, list the differences between them.

Comparing _____ and _____

Similarities

_____

Differences

_____

B. Write a paragraph.

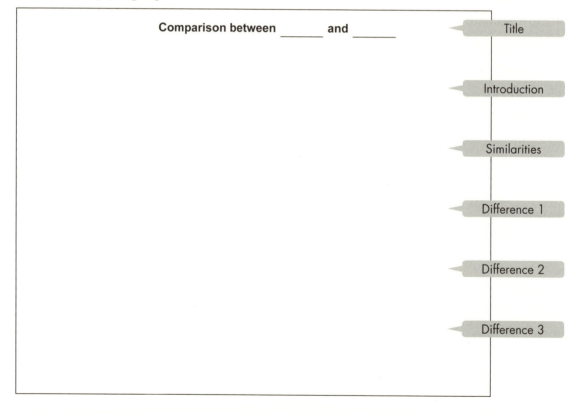

Peer Editing

Exchange your drafts and correct errors if any. Make comments to improve your partner's speech.

Describing Graphs

わかりやすいプレゼンテーションに欠かせないグラフや図の説明のしかたを練習しましょう。

💡 Getting ready

1. What kind of graph/chart would you use to show the rainfall of each month in London in 2016? (　　　　　)
2. What kind of graph/chart would you use to indicate the average hours of sleep per night of 100 people? (　　　　　)
3. What type of graph/chart would you use to describe the average global temperature over the last eight years? (　　　　　)

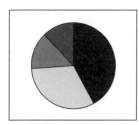

pie chart

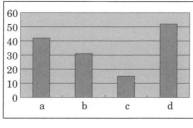

bar graph

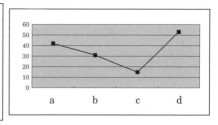

line graph

📖 Reading

Pie Charts

This pie chart shows Kenji's typical day. Look at it and fill in the blanks.

🔊 Track 17

　　This pie chart shows my typical day. I am a university student and usually have three classes a day. I (1.　　　　) about five hours at university, which (2.　　　　) for 21% of the 24 hours. I am a member of a baseball club and practice (3.　　　　) hours after classes. After that I work (4.　　　　　) for

67

three hours at a convenience store as a cashier. The club activity and part-time job takes up (5.   )% of my day. It (6.   ) an hour to go to university from my house, and I spend two hours commuting every day. When I get home, I prepare for classes and do my assignments for (7.   ) hours. Not much time is left for relaxing, but I sometimes watch videos or chat with friends on Skype. I (8.   ) six hours each night.

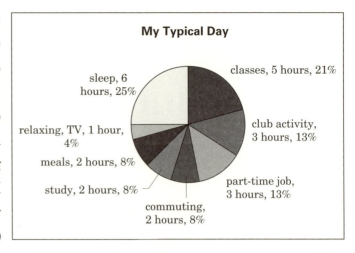

Writing

Now make your own pie chart which shows your typical day and explain it.

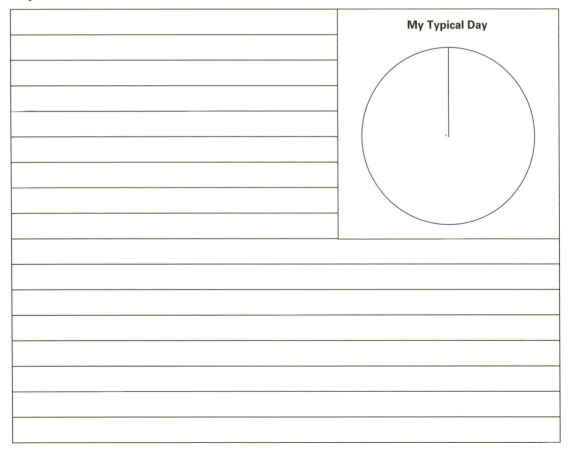

Describing Graphs

Exercise 1

Line Graphs

Describe graphs 1 to 4 in two ways, using the expressions below. Use the past tense for graphs 5 to 7.

1. Car sales

Car sales increased.
Car sales have been increasing.

2. Computer sales

Computer sales _____
Computer sales _____

3. Oil production

_____
_____

4. Coal production

_____
_____

5. Interest rates

_____

6. Consumption of beef

_____

7. Stock prices

- recover
- stabilize
- fluctuate
- increase
- decrease
- increase dramatically
- decrease dramatically

69

Exercise 2

Bar graphs

A. Look at the bar graph below and answer the questions.

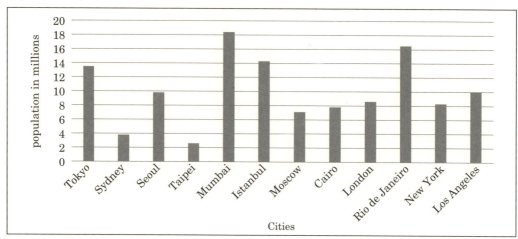

Population in big cities in 2011 to 2016

source: http://www.citypopulation.de/cities.html

1. Which city has the largest population? (   )
2. Which city has the smallest population? (   )
3. How many people live in Istanbul? (   )
4. Which city has twice as large a population as Sydney? (   )
5. In which city do more people live, Tokyo or Moscow? (   )

B. Use the bar graph again. Complete the Japanese sentences. Then, put them into English.

1. 2番目に人口の多い都市は＿＿＿＿＿＿＿です。

＿＿＿＿＿＿＿＿＿＿＿＿＿＿＿＿＿＿＿＿＿＿＿＿＿＿＿＿＿＿＿＿＿＿

2. 東京の人口は＿＿＿＿＿の人口のおよそ４分の３です。

＿＿＿＿＿＿＿＿＿＿＿＿＿＿＿＿＿＿＿＿＿＿＿＿＿＿＿＿＿＿＿＿＿＿

3. ＿＿＿＿＿と＿＿＿＿はニューヨークと同じくらいの人口を擁しています。

＿＿＿＿＿＿＿＿＿＿＿＿＿＿＿＿＿＿＿＿＿＿＿＿＿＿＿＿＿＿＿＿＿＿

C. Make three sentences based on the graph.

1. ＿＿＿＿＿＿＿＿＿＿＿＿＿＿＿＿＿＿＿＿＿＿＿＿＿＿＿＿＿＿＿＿＿
2. ＿＿＿＿＿＿＿＿＿＿＿＿＿＿＿＿＿＿＿＿＿＿＿＿＿＿＿＿＿＿＿＿＿
3. ＿＿＿＿＿＿＿＿＿＿＿＿＿＿＿＿＿＿＿＿＿＿＿＿＿＿＿＿＿＿＿＿＿

Exercise 3

A. Describe oil production in each period in the United States.

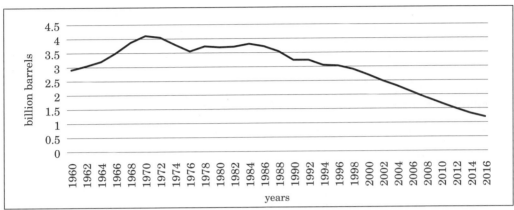

Oil production in the U.S.
data source: http://dieoff.org/42Countries/42Countries.htm

years	descriptions
1960~70	Oil production steadily increased in the 1960s.
1970	
1970~76	
1978~85	
1985~94	
1994~1998	
1998~2016	

B. Listen and fill in the blanks.

🔊 Track 18

Oil production in the United States (1. _____) in the past 30 years. This line graph shows the oil production of the United States. The x-axis (2. _____) the years while the y-axis indicates the amount of oil produced in (3. _____).

In the 1960s, oil production steadily rose from 3 billion barrels. The U.S. reached its (4. _____) of 4.1 billion barrels of oil production in 1970. After the peak, it slightly decreased to 3.8 billion barrels and (5. _____) until 1985. After 1985, it started to (6. _____). By 2016, oil production in the United States (7. _____) to 1.2 billion barrels.

Which sentence describes the general tendency of oil production? Underline the sentence.

Unit 8

📝 Prepare your speech

A. Find your own interesting graph and explain it. You can use the Internet, newspaper articles and white papers published by governmental institutions to find your graph.

☞ Key point!

When you use a graph, you need to:

1. describe the general tendency in one or two sentences.
2. explain what the x-axis and the y-axis respectively indicate.
3. explain sections of the graph in more detail.

B. Now write your paragraphs.

(First, describe the general tendency of what you are going to explain.)

This graph shows

The x-axis shows

The y-axis shows

(Give a detailed description of the graph.)

🔍 Peer Editing

Exchange your drafts and correct errors if any. Make comments to improve your partner's speech.

Unit 9

Graph Analysis

最近の気になる社会現象をグラフや表を使って英語で表現してみましょう。グラフのデータが示す数値の裏にある社会的背景を分析してみましょう。

Getting ready

A. Put into Japanese.

1. increase　　　　＿＿＿＿＿＿
2. rise rapidly　　　＿＿＿＿＿＿
3. gradually　　　　＿＿＿＿＿＿
4. slightly　　　　　＿＿＿＿＿＿

B. Put into English.

1. 年々　　　　　　　　　＿＿＿＿＿＿
2. 高い状態が続く　　　　＿＿＿＿＿＿
3. 〜の間中ずっと　　　　＿＿＿＿＿＿
4. 急落する　　　　　　　＿＿＿＿＿＿
5. 劇的な急落を記録する　＿＿＿＿＿＿
6. 一定のままである　　　＿＿＿＿＿＿

Unit 9

🎧 Listening 1

First listening

Look at the graph below, listen to the statement and write down the reason why the birth rate suddenly dropped in 1966.

 Track 19

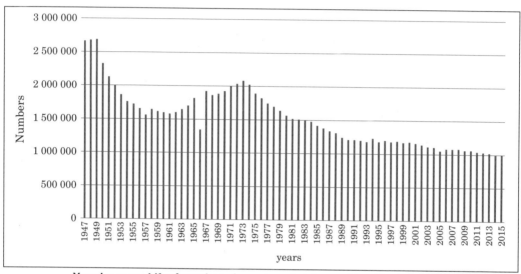

Year-by-year shift of number of new born babies and total fertility rates
Created based on http://www.mhlw.go.jp/toukei/saikin/hw/jinkou/geppo/nengai16/dl/h1.pdf
Note: Okinawa Prefecture is not included in the figures for 1972 and before.

Reason :

_____
_____
_____
_____
_____

Second listening

Listen again and fill in the blanks. Then translate each sentence into Japanese.

🔊 Track 19

1. This graph (　　　　) the number of newborn babies in Japan (　　　　) 1947 (　　　) 2015.

Graph Analysis

2. The birthrate was at a record (　　　) between (　　　) and (　　　).

3. The number of newborn babies (　　　) to (　　　) year by year in the 1950s.

4. The number of babies (　　　) to (　　　) again (　　　) the 1960s and the early 1970s.

5. The birth rate (　　　) its second (　　　) between 1971 and 1974.

6. In 1966, the graph (　　　) a dramatic (　　　) as compared to the (　　　) and (　　　) years.

7. It was because (　　) an old (　　　) (　　　) women who were born in a particular year.

8. In 1966, people were still (　　　　) about the superstition and (　　) (　　　) babies.

Look at the graph again and discuss the questions below with your partner.

1. What do you think is the reason for women having fewer children after 1973?

   _____

2. Since 1980, the fertility rate has been declining. Consider other possible causes of the lower birth rate.

   _____
   _____
   _____

Listening 2

Vocabulary preview

Put into English.

1. 家庭、世帯 _____
2. 日中に _____
3. 電力消費量 _____
4. 待機時消費電力 _____
5. 電力使用が集中しない時間帯 _____

Look at the graph below. Then listen to the statement and answer the following questions.

Track 20

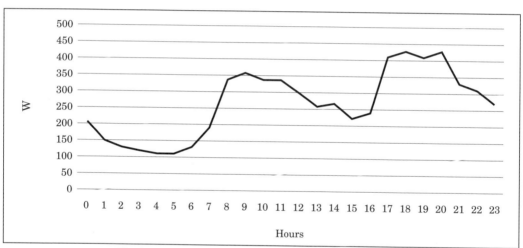

The Pattern of Average Daily Electricity Use in October
Reference: http://standard-project.net/energy/statistics/energy-consumption-day.html

1. What is the graph about?
   _____

2. Why is the consumption of electricity low between 1 p.m. and 4 p.m.?
   _____

3. Why is the consumption of electricity the highest between 5 p.m. and 8 p.m.?
   _____

4. What can we do to save electricity? Write down your own idea.

Graph Analysis

_____
_____
_____
_____
_____
_____
_____
_____

📖 Reading

Read the graph and the passage below and complete the outline of the passage.

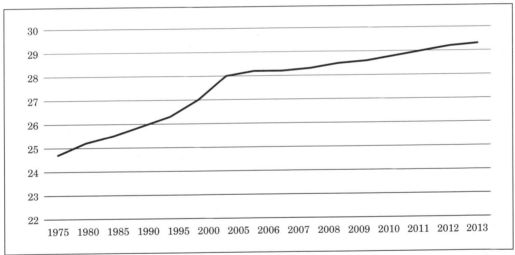

The average age at first marriage for women in Japan

Created based on http://www8.cao.go.jp/shoushi/shoushika/whitepaper/measures/w-2015/27webhonpen/html/b1_s1-1-3.html downloaded on 28th August, 2017

🔊 Track 21

  This graph shows the average age for the first marriage of women in Japan from 1975 to 2013. Since 1975, the average age has been constantly rising. There was a sharp rise between 1995 and 2005. Then the average age continued to rise year by year since 2005. Why has the average age been rising? The high employment rate of women may be one of the causes. For Japanese women in their late 20s and early 30s, marriage is not the main concern in life any more.

Nowadays, stable jobs are important for many women. Another reason might be the unequal share of housework between a husband and a wife. Some women worry that they will have to take care of most of the housework, besides working outside. Such changes in their attitude towards life and their working styles seem to affect the average age of their first marriage.

<Outline>
Introduction: What is the graph about?

_____
_____

Body:
1. Describe the graph.

_____
_____
_____

2. Give two possible causes of the change.
    a. _____
    b. _____

Conclusion:

_____
_____

Graph Analysis

 Prepare your speech

Find a graph and write your own speech following the format below.

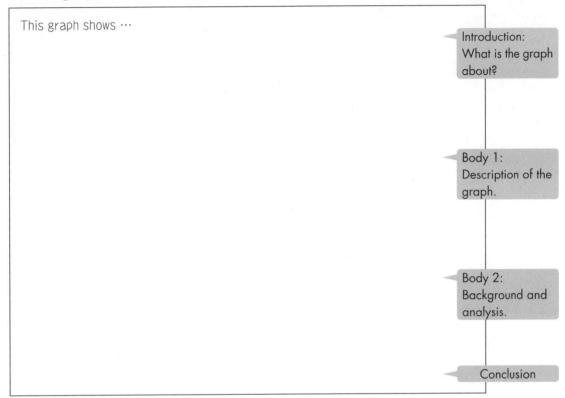

 Peer Editing

Exchange your drafts and correct errors if any. Make comments to improve your partner's speech.

Unit 10

Research and Presentation 1: Comparing Two Rival Companies

グラフや表の説明、2つの事柄の比較などを応用して、自分で調べたデータをもとに、2つの企業を比較するプレゼンテーションをしましょう。

Getting ready

Which two companies/brands/teams compete with each other?

Types of industries / institutions	Rivals	
Car manufacturers	Toyota	Nissan
Fast food shops		
Convenience stores		
Clothing stores		
Coffee shop chains		
Airlines		
Courier firms (宅配便)		
Mobile phone companies		
Baseball teams		
Newspapers		

80

Exercise

A. If you compare two convenience stores, on what aspects will you compare them?

1. Numbers of shops: how many shops are there in Japan?
2. Amount of sales: how much sales revenue did the company generate last year?
3. _____
4. _____
5. _____
6. _____
7. _____
8. _____
9. _____
10. _____

B. By using graphs and charts, in which aspects would you compare the two companies?

_____

Listening

Vocabulary preview

Put Japanese into English and put English into Japanese.

1. 主要な	_____	2. _____	the number of ~
3. 従業員	the number of _____	4. 売り上げ	_____
5. _____	one billion	6. 100億	_____
7. 1000億	_____	8. _____	1000 billion / one trillion
9. _____	level off	10. 複合企業体	conglomerate
11. 製造する	_____	12. _____	in addition to ~
13. 顧客	_____	14. 照準を合わせる	target

First Listening

Listen to the comparison of two companies. Fill in the blanks and complete the chart. Then, answer the questions. Graphs are on the next page.

🔊 Track 22

The speaker is comparing _____ and _____.

	7-Eleven	Lawson
Market share	The largest	
Number of stores		13,111
Number of ( )		9,400
Sales in 2016	4,500 billion yen	
Sales per store	230 million yen	( ) yen
Have sales been increasing or decreasing in the past 5 years?	They have been ( ).	They have been increasing but have a levelling-off period every few years.

1. For which aspect did the speaker use graphs?

   _____

2. Which aspect did the speaker explain in detail?

   _____

Research and Presentation 1: Comparing Two Rival Companies

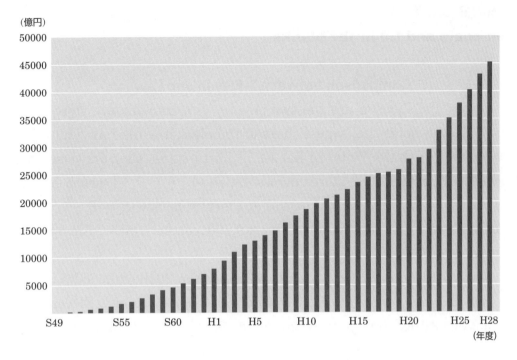

Graph 1 Sales of 7-Eleven

(株)セブン-イレブン・ジャパン　http://www.sej.co.jp/company/suii.html retrieved on 24th August, 2017

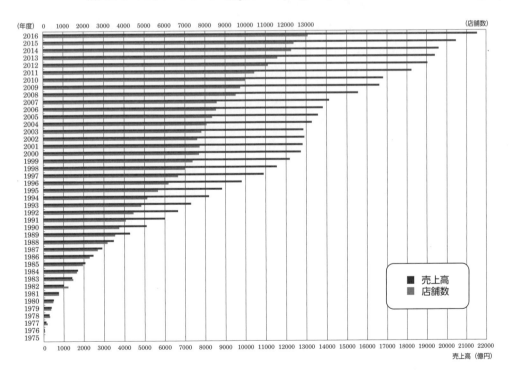

Graph 2 Sales of Lawson

http://www.lawson.co.jp/company/corporate/data/sales/ retrieved on 6th August 2017

Second listening

Listen again and fill in the blanks.

🔊 Track 22

Comparison between 7-Eleven and Lawson

7-Eleven and Lawson are the two (1. _____) convenience store chains in Japan. 7-Eleven holds the largest share of the market while Lawson has (2. _____) share. 7-eleven has (3. _____) stores than Lawson. In 2017, 7-Eleven had about 19,638 stores across Japan (4. _____) Lawson had 13,111 stores. (5. _____) employees at Lawson, however, is (6. _____) than that of 7-Eleven: Lawson employs about 9,400 people while 7-Eleven employs 8,600 people.

Sales at 7-Eleven (7. _____) 4,500 billion yen in 2016 while sales at Lawson were just (8. _____) of that. The average sales per store of 7-Eleven was 230 million yen while that of Lawson was (9. _____) million yen. Graph 1 (10. _____) sales of 7-Eleven; sales have been steadily increasing over the past 25 years, and have notably increased from 2,700 billion to 3,500 billion yen (11. _____) the years 2008 and 2012. On the other hand, Lawson seems to have (12. _____) every few years. Graph 2 shows sales of Lawson; they have been increasing in the last three years. Between 2009 and 2010 and between 2013 and 2014, however, they levelled off.

Since 7-Eleven is a part of a conglomerate, Seven and I Holdings, the store chains have their own products developed by their associated companies. 7-Eleven sells a lot of soft drinks and snacks from their own (13. _____). The prices of these products are (14. _____), and yet the quality and taste are as good as those of products manufactured by other established brands. On the other hand, Lawson is trying to increase their customers by making three types of shops. In addition to the ordinary type of Lawson, they have introduced Lawson 100, selling fresh foods and Natural Lawson, which (15. _____) customers who prefer healthy, natural food.

Structure of the passage

1st paragraph

_____

_____

2nd paragraph

_____

3rd paragraph

_____

📝 Prepare your speech

Start your research by using the Internet or reading books and newspapers.

1. Companies/organizations compared:

2. What aspects are compared?
    a.
    b.
    c.
    d.
    e.

3. For which aspects do you use graphs and charts?

4. What is a noticeable difference between the two companies?

🔍 Peer Editing

Exchange your drafts and correct errors if any. Make comments to improve your partner's speech.

Before your presentation

Check your script and practice:

<words and numbers>

1. Are the companies' names accurate?
2. Can you pronounce the large numbers correctly and fluently?
3. Can you read years such as 2017 and 2010?
4. Do you have any difficulty in pronouncing some words in your script? If you do, do you want to change them for other words easier to pronounce?

<using graphs>

1. For which aspects do you use the graphs/charts?
2. Can you explain what the x-axis and y-axis indicate while pointing at each one?

Unit 11

Research and Presentation 2: Problems and Solutions

問題解決のためにはまず、原因を見極めて、解決策を考え、アクションを起こすことが必要です。Part I では身の回りにある様々な問題をリサーチし、解決策を提示するポスター発表を、Part II では、さらに社会的な課題をポスター形式で共同発表をする練習してみましょう。

Part I
Analyzing a problem and suggesting solutions

Getting ready

In order to solve a problem, you need to analyze it from a variety of angles and identify the causes or reasons. Study the example.

Example Problem

Tourists are destroying a beautiful flower garden. They step into the garden to take pictures.

☞ Problem solution

Step 1. Brainstorming: Think of the background and why this is happening.
- increase of international tourists
- photos for SNS
- signs in Japanese

Step 2. Identify the causes and reasons

Tourists want to take photos at this beautiful flower garden as a souvenir of their trip. There may be no sign saying "Keep out!" in other languages and they don't know where to get good photo shoots.

Step 3. Ideas for solution

Put up a sign saying "Keep out" in several foreign languages.

Put up a sign "Photo spot" at a nice spot where the flowers won't be harmed.

Unit 11

Now, work with your group members to solve the following problems.

Problem 1. I often drop my smartphone and the screen gets cracked.

Step 1. Brainstorming: Think of the background and why this is happening.

_____

_____

Step 2. Identify the causes or reasons

_____

_____

Step 3. Ideas for solution

_____

_____

Problem 2. Japanese traditional crafts such as *kiriko* glass or kimono textile are gradually disappearing.

Step 1. Brainstorming: Think of the background and why this is happening.

_____

_____

_____

_____

Step 2. Identify the causes and reasons

_____

_____

_____

_____

_____

Step 3. Ideas for solution

_____

_____

_____

_____

_____

_____

Research and Presentation 2: Problems and Solutions

🎧 Listening

A. Listen to the conversation and fill in the blanks. Then answer the questions.

🔊 Track 23

Matt: We are having such (1. _____) lately. We have never had such hot days as this at this time of the year.

Mimi: I know. Yesterday's rain was so dreadful. Many roads in my neighborhood were totally flooded. My grandmother said she has never seen anything like this in this town since her childhood.

Matt: We may need to prepare for even more severe weather.

Mimi: Oh, I am scared. Can't we do something about it? Why is it happening?

Matt: Many scientists believe it (2. _____) global warming. The (3. _____) of global warming is CO_2 emissions from our daily life.

Mimi: I see, but the problem seems so big and I don't see any (4. _____). Do you think we can do something on an individual level?

Matt: Well, CO_2 is emitted by burning (5. _____) such as oil and coal to produce products or electricity to make our lives convenient. So, I am sure each of us can do something to (6. _____).

Mimi: OK. How about using less electricity a day? Turning off the TV when not watching? …Well, but this does not help much, does it?

Matt: Why don't we ask all our classmates to do the same? 50 students can (7. _____).

Mimi: That's right! Spreading the word and reminding people are very important. You are great! Do you have any other ideas to share with our classmates?

Matt: _____

1. What problem are they talking about?

2. What is one of the causes of the problem?

3. What solutions are suggested?

4. What would Matt say in the last line? Think of a solution and write it down.

89

B. Then, share your idea with your classmates and take notes.

Your classmates' ideas for solutions:

Research

A. 興味ある問題について、① **background** (背景、具体的な事例、状況などのデータ)、
② **causes** についてリサーチしてみましょう。

List of possible topics
- endangered species
- obesity
- *karoshi* (death from overwork)
- shortage of child care centers
- shrinking glaciers
- increase of unmarried people
- other topics _____

Example

Topic: Endangered species

The numbers of animals, plants and insects listed as endangered species are increasing rapidly. Before 1975, only one species became extinct per year, but currently more than 40,000 species become extinct a year.

There are several causes. The major cause is the destruction of their habitat by human beings. Some other causes are illegal hunting and introductions of exotic species which can give serious impact on native ecosystem.

Source: https://www.env.go.jp/nature/yasei/ex-situ/step0.html

Your research

Topic: _____

_____
_____
_____
_____
_____

Source: _____

B. Now write down your research results on a poster sheet (size depending on the size of your audience) and show and explain your research results to your group members or classmates. The sheet should look like this:

Problem:

- Background / condition / status / example (use data of your research)

- Cause / reasons

- Suggested Solutions

- Reference

Part II

Prepare a group poster presentation

後半では、SDG (Sustainable Developmental Goals) についてグループでリサーチし、解決策を提案してみましょう。

Vocabulary

Match English expressions with Japanese. These are some of the Sustainable Developmental Goals.

1. gender equality (　　)
2. healthy lives (　　)
3. well-being (　　)
4. hunger (　　)
5. food security (　　)
6. nutrition (　　)
7. sustainable agriculture (　　)
8. inclusive and quality education (　　)
9. lifelong learning (　　)

ア　栄養
イ　生涯学習
ウ　福祉
エ　男女平等
オ　食料安全
カ　飢餓
キ　健康的な生活
ク　包括的で質の高い教育
ケ　持続可能な農業

💬 Discussion

A. Make a group of 3 or 4 students. Then find a topic from below.

List of possible topics
1. Achieve gender equality and empower all women and girls.
2. Ensure healthy lives and promote well-being for all ages.
3. End hunger, achieve food security and improved nutrition and promote sustainable agriculture.
4. Ensure inclusive and quality education for all and promote lifelong learning.
5. Other: _____
   Your Group Topic: _____

B. Discuss with your group members. Why should we care?

C. Do some research and discuss more.
1. As a homework, each member should find articles related to the topic.
2. Share the information with others.
   Briefly summarize and tell the members the contents giving the keywords in the article. You can explain it in English or Japanese, or in both. Try to understand the background of the problems.
3. Based on the research, discuss possible solutions.

📝 Prepare your poster presentation

A. Prepare the contents.
1. Decide four or five keywords which explain your presentation well.
2. Check the sources. What are the titles of the articles? Where do they come from?
3. Decide the outline of presentation: Introduction, Body, and Conclusion.

B. Make a poster.
1. Decide who is responsible for each part of the presentation. If there are four members in a group, each member can be assigend to do Introduction (1 student), Body (2 students), and Conclusion (1 student).

Research and Presentation 2: Problems and Solutions

2. Write a draft. Here are some tips for making your poster look attractive:
(i) Pick up the keywords of your part, and make the sentences short and simple. Listing up is easier for the audience to understand.
(ii) Please include diagrams, figures, pictures, and photos. (See Unit 8 and 9 for making graphs).
3. Integrate each of your members' parts into one poster.

Now, you are ready to present your poster with your group members.

_____ ◀ Title

Keywords: _____ _____ _____ _____

Introduction: the objectives (the title) and a brief outline of your presentation

◀ Introduction

Body 1: problems (supported by the background behind the problems, etc.)

◀ Body 1

Body 2: solutions (supported by what are currently being done and what can be done with possible future approaches, etc.)

◀ Body 2

Conclusion: a summary of presentations, future suggestions, etc.

◀ Conclusion

🔍 Peer Editing

Exchange your drafts and correct errors if any. Make comments to improve your partner's speech.

Unit 12
Research and Presentation 3: Organ Transplants

ある社会的テーマに関して賛否とその理由を英語で表現することを学びましょう。ここでは臓器移植の問題を取り上げます。

 Getting ready

Already carry a card?

1. Do you know where you can get this card? Are there any other way to express your wish to donate your organs?
   _____
   _____
   _____
   _____

2. Do you have this card? Do you know anyone who has this card?
   _____
   _____
   _____
   _____

Vocabulary

Study the words and phrases relating to organ transplants. Match English expressions with Japanese.

1. surgery (　　)
2. insurance (　　)
3. gift of life (　　)
4. blood donation (　　)
5. rejection (　　)
6. donate (　　)
7. brain death (　　)
8. donor (　　)
9. recipient (　　)

ア 命の贈り物
イ 臓器提供者
ウ 拒絶反応
エ 提供する
オ 保険
カ 手術
キ 献血
ク 臓器をもらう人
ケ 脳死

Research

Get information from the Internet or books to find out about the following issues.

1. What is the latest situation in Japan with regard to organ transplants?

    a. Who can become an organ donor? Can children donate after their death?

    _____
    _____
    _____
    _____

    b. Can people buy or sell organs?

    _____
    _____

    c. What organs can be transplanted?

    _____
    _____

2. Why do so many patients go abroad to receive an organ transplant?

    _____
    _____

Useful websites for your research

(公社)日本臓器移植ネットワーク・ホームページ http://www.jotnw.or.jp/ (日)
国立循環器病研究センターによる臓器提供シミュレーションの実施内容 http://www.ncvc.go.jp/transplant/simulation/index.html (日)
UNOS http://www.unos.org/ (米)

Reading

Read the article below and answer the following questions.

The common transplants include hearts, lungs, livers, pancreases, kidneys, small intestines, bones, skins and corneas. Some organs and tissues can be donated by living donors, such as a kidney or part of the liver.

According to the World Health Organization (WHO), only a few countries such as Pakistan and Romania do not accept brain death as actual death. In Japan, the 1997 Organ Transplant Law legalized brain-dead donor transplants for the first time. However, only a limited number of organ transplants from brain-dead people were conducted between 1997 and 2010 — only 86 cases in 13 years!

The number of transplants from the brain-dead was very small in Japan partly due to the organ transplant rules. Before the organs of a brain-dead person can be removed for transplantation, the donor must have expressed their will to be a donor while he or she was alive. Without the donor's written consent, no organ transplant can be carried out. Moreover, a donor's family can cancel the donor's written consent.

In 2010, the revised Law on Organ Transplants took effect. Under the revised law, organs can be removed from brain-dead donors by their families' consent. What's more, children under 15 can donate their organs. After the revision of the law, the number of organ transplantations from brain-dead donors increased — about 60 cases in one year. But still, the number is very small compared with the United States, where about 92 transplants take place each day on average.

Meanwhile, organ donation policies vary across the world. Japan currently uses an opt-in system. With this system, people have to sign up to a register to donate their organs after death. On the other hand, with an opt-out system, only those who object to donating their organs have to register to be on the non-donation list.

Wales introduced this opt-out system in 2016 and only 6 % of adults opposed themselves to donation. Spain, France, Belgium, Ireland and Finland use this opt-out system and they all have between 70-120 % more donors than England.

Social media is an effective tool to make more people register as donors. According to Johns Hopkins researchers, Facebook is boosting the number of organ donors. There were 13,012 new online donor registrations on the first day they began the initiative. It was a 21.2-fold increase over the average daily registration rate of 616 in the US.

☐lung 肺 ☐liver 肝臓 ☐pancreas すい臓 ☐kidney 腎臓 ☐intestines 腸 ☐cornea 角膜 ☐legalize 合法化する ☐conduct 実施する ☐will 意志 ☐written consent 承諾書 ☐take effect 施行する ☐opt-in 選んで(臓器提供を)する ☐opt-out 選んで(臓器提供を)しない ☐oppose 反対する ☐21.2-fold 21.2倍

1. Which countries refuse to accept brain death as actual death?
   _____

2. How many people donated their organs under the old Organ Transplant Law, between 1997 and 2010?
   _____

3. In the United States, how many organ transplants take place every day?
   _____

4. Why is the number of organ transplants from the brain-dead so small in Japan? Give two reasons.
   a. _____
   _____
   b. _____

5. Give two effective ideas which can increase the number of organ donors.
   _____

Unit 12

🎧 Listening 1

First listening

Listen to the news report and fill in the blanks.

🔊 Track 25

Bill Conner suddenly lost his 20-year old daughter five months ago. Abbey and her brother, Austin, 23, were found (1.　　　　) at the bottom of a pool in Cancun. Austin survived, but Abbey was declared (2.　　　　).

Abbey had registered to be an (3.　　　　) when she got her driver's license. Her father decided to donate his beloved daughter's organs. Her organs saved four lives, from the ages of 20 to 60. Her eyes and other tissues were given to other (4.　　　　) as well.

After five months from Abbey's sudden death, Conner decided to travel by bicycle from Madison to Florida and (5.　　　　) people to register as donors. He needed to do something positive to (6.　　　　) his great loss. But at the same time, he had another purpose — to meet Jack in Louisiana. He was saved by Abbey's heart.

The (7.　　　　) center that handled Abbey's organs sent letters to all the recipients and asked if they'd be interested in meeting Abbey's father. One of the recipients, Jack (8.　　　　). He had had a heart attack and his heart was quickly (9.　　　　). He was given 10 days to live before he received Abbey's donation.

When Conner met Jack, he felt like he knew him already. Jack gave him a stethoscope and Conner listened to his daughter's (10.　　　　) inside his chest. His family had recorded the sound of Jack's heart so Conner could listen to them at any time.

Bill Conner continued on his journey to share his daughter's story and encourage people to register as organ donors.

☐unconscious 意識不明　☐beloved daughter 愛する娘　☐misfortune 不幸　☐stethoscope 聴診器

Second listening

Listen to the news report again and answer the following questions.

🔊 Track 25

1. When did Abbey register to be an organ donor?

Research and Presentation 3: Organ Transplants

2. How many people did Abbey's organs save?

3. Why did Bill Conner travel by bicycle from Madison to Florida?

4. Why did Jack gave a stethoscope to Bill?

Listening 2

First listening

Listen to the news report and fill in the blanks.

Track 26

A fisheries company executive, Suzuo Yamashita, 59, in Matsuyama, had been suffering from diabetes (1.   ). He desperately wanted to have a kidney for transplant. He was on the waiting list for a transplant, but his chances were very small, as 11 thousand other patients were also waiting for kidney (2.   ). None of his family or friends agreed to be a (3.   ).

His common-law wife, Tomoko Matsushita, 60, was (4.   ) her husband. She knew a 59-year-old woman who was a landlord in Matsuyama. An idea occurred to her. "How about asking the woman to sell her kidney to us?"

To the couple (5.   ) a great idea. Suzuo and Tomoko visited the woman and asked her if she could give Suzuo one of her kidneys, offering 300,000 yen and a brand new car. After some thoughts, the woman (6.   ) give her kidney in exchange for the money and the car.

A few weeks after their transplant (7.   ), the police found that the woman had sold her kidney to Suzuo. The couple and the woman donor became the first to be convicted under the 1997 law that bans the buying and selling of (8.   ) for transplants. The couple were found guilty and sentenced to suspended one-year prison terms. The donor was not indicted on criminal charges but was fined 1 million yen.

☐fishery 水産業 ☐executive 経営者 ☐suffer from 〜を患う ☐diabetes 糖尿病 ☐desperately want to 〜を心底欲している ☐patient 患者 ☐common-law wife 内縁の妻 ☐landlord 地主 ☐in exchange for 〜の見返りに ☐convict 有罪判決を下す ☐ban 禁止する ☐find guilty 有罪とする ☐be sentenced to 〜刑を言い渡される ☐suspended prison term 執行猶予刑 ☐be indicted on 〜で起訴される ☐criminal charges 刑事罰 ☐be fined 〜の罰金を課せられる

Second listening

Listen to the news report again and answer the following questions.

🔊 Track 26

1. Why did Suzuo Yamashita need an organ transplant?

2. Who agreed to give Suzuo his/her kidney?

3. Did the donor receive any reward in exchange for his/her organ? What did he/she get?

4. Who were found guilty in the court, the recipient, the donor or both?

5. Which one of the following is illegal according to Japanese law? (   )
    a. receiving a kidney
    b. giving a kidney
    c. paying money to the donor
    d. performing an organ transplant operation

💬 Discussion 1

1. Do you think Mr. Yamashita was given an appropriate sentence? Was it too light or too heavy?

Research and Presentation 3: Organ Transplants

2. How can we solve a shortage of donors/donated organs? Give your own ideas.

_____
_____
_____
_____
_____
_____

3. If your family member needs a kidney, would you be a donor? Why or why not?

_____
_____

Discussion 2

A. The following are various opinions on organ transplants from different standpoints. Whose viewpoint does each statement represent? Write D for donors' viewpoint, R for recipients', DF for donor's families', and O for the opposed. Many of the statements represent more than one point of view.

1. I am for organ transplants and I want to become a donor because I can save lives. (　　)
2. I would feel uncomfortable with someone's kidney inside me. (　　)
3. I would appreciate donations if I were a patient. (　　)
4. I would donate my organ to save my child. (　　)
5. I feel sorry for patients who have been waiting for organ transplantation for a long time. (　　)
6. I would be a brain-dead donor but I wouldn't be a living donor. (　　)
7. I think I would feel less pain because I know that I can help someone to live a longer and healthier life. (　　)
8. A shortage of organs for transplant is a serious problem. (　　)
9. I would receive an organ transplant if I needed one, but I would not buy organs from others. (　　)
10. I would like to be a donor but I am against the selling of organs because life

should be a gift, not a purchase. (　)
11. Your donor might have some diseases. (　)
12. There could be medical risks with removing an organ from a living donor. (　)
13. I think organ transplants are destroying our souls and human values. (　)
14. I am against organ transplants, because a large black market for organs could develop. (　)
15. I don't want to have an organ transplant in order to live longer. (　)
16. I cannot be a donor because all surgery can cause some pain while recovering. (　)
17. Crimes like fake marriage and kidnapping children can increase because of a shortage of organs. (　)
18. I would feel bad if my family member donated his / her organs to someone else. (　)
19. It must be nice that I could give someone the gift of life after I die. (　)
20. My son's gift offered a second chance of life to 5 people. (　)

B. Add your own opinions to the statements above.

_____
_____
_____
_____

C. Use the expressions above and share your opinion about organ transplants with your group members. Keep the conversation going in the group by using "Agreeing" and "Softeners" from the Useful Expressions (see pp.13-14).

Example:

A: I think I would be a donor because I feel sorry for patients who have been waiting for organ transplantation for a long time.

B: <u>I'm with you.</u> It must be nice that I would give someone the gift of life after I die. ^(Agreeing)

C: <u>I understand what you're saying, but</u> I cannot be a donor because all surgery can cause some pain while recovering. ^(Softeners)

Research and Presentation 3: Organ Transplants

D: <u>You're right.</u> There could be medical risks with removing an organ from a living donor.

A: <u>I hate to disagree with you, but</u> I think I would feel less pain because I know that I can help someone to live a longer and healthier life.

📝 Prepare your speech

Write your speech by using the words or phrases that are presented in this unit.

List of possible topics

1. Would you give permission for your organs to be donated after death or brain-death?
2. Would you donate your kidney if one of your family members needed a kidney transplant?
3. Would you accept an organ transplant if you had serious diabetes?
4. Would you agree to his/her decision if your relative wished to donate his/her organs to someone?
5. How can we solve the shortage of donors/donated organs?

_____   ◀ Title

Introductionではこれから何を話すのかを明確に述べます。聴衆に問いかけたり、印象に残るような事柄を入れると魅力的な導入部となり、聞き手を自分の主張へと引き込むことが出来ます。   ◀ Introduction

・Do you know what percentage of people have expressed their wish to donate their organs in Japan?

・According to the newspaper, only two percent of Japanese show willingness to donate their organs.

・If a member of my family needed a kidney, I would be a donor. And I have three reasons.

103

Unit 12

BodyではIntroductionで述べた自分の主張をサポートする論拠をここで述べます。
・Let me tell you why I think so. Firstly, ... Secondly, ... Thirdly, ... ◀ Body: Reasons

Conclusionは締めの部分です。自分の意見が明白に相手に伝わるように、整理して結びの段落を書きましょう。 ◀ Conclusion

🔍 Peer Editing

Exchange your drafts and correct errors if any. Make comments to improve your partner's speech.

Unit 13

Pros and Cons of Capital Punishment

ある命題に対して、自分が賛成か、反対か立場を明らかにして、その理由を述べる練習をしましょう。ここでは、死刑制度の存続について考えていきます。

Getting ready

What do you know about capital punishment? Discuss in your class.

1. List of methods: how is the death penalty carried out?

    By _____
    _____

2. What crimes can be punished by the death penalty?

    _____
    _____
    _____

3. Which countries retain capital punishment and which countries abolished it?

    _____
    _____
    _____
    _____

Listening 1

Before you listen: what do you think?

The number of countries that retain the death penalty has been (　　　　　　).

First listening

Listen and fill in the table.

🔊 Track 27

	2006	2016
Number of countries that have abolished capital punishment		
Number of countries which retain capital punishment		

Second listening

Listen and complete the sentences. You can also use the table above.

🔊 Track 27

1. By 2006, 129 countries _____ while _____.

2. Ten years later the number of countries that had abolished capital punishment was _____ while _____.

🎧 Listening 2

Vocabulary preview

Put into English.

1. 死刑　_____
2. 廃止する　_____　　3. 維持する　_____
4. 増える　_____　　　5. 減る　_____
6. 終身刑　_____　　　7. 代わりの方法　_____
8. 仮釈放　_____　　　9. 殺人の発生率　_____

Listen to the dialogue and fill in the blanks. Then, listen to five statements. Write T if the statement matches the dialogue and write F if it does not.

🔊 Track 28

Chika: Mike, you're from (1. _____), aren't you?
Mike: Yes. From Montreal.
Chika: Does Canada have the death (2. _____)?
Mike: No. We (3. _____) it.
Chika: Didn't the murder rate (4. _____) up after you stopped it?

Mike: No. it went down, interestingly.
Chika: Why did you abolish capital (5.   )?
Mike: We felt there was an (6.   ) to the death penalty.
Chika: Like (7.   ) sentence without parole?
Mike: Exactly.

1. (   )   2. (   )   3. (   )   4. (   )   5. (   )

Exercise 1

Put into English.

1. いくつかの国は死刑を廃止しました。

2. 死刑の代替として仮釈放のない終身刑があります。

3. 死刑の廃止後、カナダでは殺人の発生率は減少しました。

Listening 3

First listening

Listen and choose the name of the country for each pie chart and fill in the blanks.

Track 29

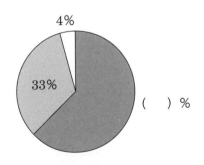

Support and opposition to capital punishment in (US / Japan) in 2014

4%
33%
(   ) %

■ favor ■ not in favor □ no opinion

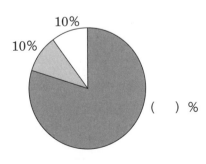

Support and opposition to capital punishment in (US / Japan) in 2014

10%
10%
(   ) %

■ favor ■ not in favor □ no opinion

Created based on: http://www.gallup.com/poll/1606/death-penalty.aspx downloaded on 30 August, 2017.
Created based on: http://survey.gov-online.go.jp/h26/h26-houseido/zh/z02.html downloaded on 30 August, 2017.

Unit 13

Second listening

Listen and put each sentence into English. Use the present tense. (現在形で)

🔊 Track 29

1. 日本では8割の人が死刑制度を支持しています。

   In Japan, _____
   _____

2. アメリカでは33%の人が死刑制度に反対しています。

   In the United States, _____
   _____
   _____
   _____
   _____

Not all the states in the U.S. retain the death penalty. Check on the Internet:

1. How many states have abolished the death penalty in the United States? (   )

2. How many states retain capital punishment? (   )

💬 Discussion

Make groups of four or five people and discuss:

1. Why have so many countries abolished the death penalty?

   _____
   _____
   _____
   _____
   _____
   _____

2. Why do some countries including Japan retain capital punishment?

   _____
   _____
   _____

Reading

Students are discussing issues about the death penalty. Do they agree or disagree with the death penalty? Check the appropriate box in the table below with regard to each speaker's opinion.

🔊 Track 30

Kazuhiro: Do you believe that the death penalty should be in use in society or is it a cruel and unusual punishment?

Yoshiya: Some people say that capital punishment prevents other murders, but I don't think it is the best way to prevent murder. Murders take place in the heat of action. They are often committed by people who know their victims. I just can't imagine a murderer thinking about the effects of his killing. Real cold-blooded killers think themselves too clever to be caught.

Rie: By sentencing someone to death, you don't prevent other murderers from committing their crimes, but at least you stop this very individual you've sentenced to death from committing another crime.

Kazuma: Criminals should pay the penalty for their sin. If the criminal has taken someone's life, the only way that the murderer can pay for his terrible act is with his own life.

Ryuji: I can't agree more. If someone traps and tortures others for fun, the death penalty is a mercy thrown upon them. If the essence of "an eye for an eye" stayed true, the family members would capture the murderer and do the same thing twice over.

Kei: It is illogical to blame a murderer and then do the same as an act of revenge. What you do is commit a murder as well, and the only difference is that you do it legally.

Koki: I agree with Kei. It's odd that people seem to think that an eye for an eye is right in the case of murder, but in no other crimes. We don't rape the rapist, assault those who have assaulted others. If you were convicted of knocking someone's tooth out, you would not be punished by having your tooth pulled out.

Haruka: The only good reason for the death penalty I can think of is that it will give back a sense of justice to the victim's family and friends. Still, the victim of the crime won't come back to life again anyway.

Takashi: As long as the death penalty is maintained, there is always the danger that innocent people will be executed because of errors in the criminal justice system. A convict could be forced to say anything under torture, even confess to a crime s/he didn't commit. Unfair trials can result in killing innocent people.

Shintaro: We should look for other ways which might stop people from committing crimes. Instead of the death penalty, we could give them life imprisonment without parole.

Masami: There is always a possibility that a murderer will repent of his crime. Such a person might even become a model citizen. A new chance for life should be given even to murderers.

	agree	disagree	ambiguous
Kazuhiro	chair		
Yoshiya			
Rie			
Kazuma			
Ryuji			
Kei			
Koki			
Haruka			
Takashi			
Shintaro			
Masami			

Exercise 2

Choose expressions from the lists below and fill in the blanks. After that, work in pairs and play the roles of pro-person and con-person in turn.

Pros and Cons of Capital Punishment

Proposition: Japan Needs Capital Punishment

Pros

1. Certain crimes are so (   ) that executing the criminal is the only way to respond.
2. If a person violates someone's right to life, the person should be (   ) by the death penalty.
3. Some people say that (   ) people can be killed by capital punishment, but the number of such cases is very small compared with the number of murders (   ) by the death penalty.
4. It is the only way to (   ) the victim's family.
5. Some criminals cannot be rehabilitated. They never (   ) what they did and repeat the same thing as long as they live.
6. Life imprisonment (   ). Keeping a prisoner for fifty years in a prison costs more than twice as much as the death penalty.
7. Capital punishment can (   ) murder.

| costs | punished | innocent | repent | awful | prevented | satisfy | prevent |

Cons

1. The death penalty is a cruel punishment. Taking human life is morally (   ) under any circumstances.
2. The death penalty (   ) the right to life.
3. Once an innocent life is lost, it cannot be (   ).
4. Even if the criminal is punished by the death penalty, the victims will never come back to (   ).
5. Criminals, even murderers, can be (   ).
6. Capital punishment costs. The costs of trials and (   ) for a capital case are greater than those of other cases.
7. Capital punishment (   ) prevent murder.

| life | appeals | wrong | violates | rehabilitated | cannot | recovered |

Prepare your speech

このユニットで考察したことをもとに proposition に対する自分の立場を明らかにした上で、スピーチの原稿を用意しましょう。

Proposition：Japan needs capital punishment.

> これから死刑問題について話す旨を伝える。聴衆に問いかけたり、印象に残るような事柄を入れたりすると魅力的な導入部となる。 ◀ **Introduction**
> ・Have you ever thought about the feelings of the victim's family?
> ・Do you know of a recent murder case in which the defendant was sentenced to death?
> ・The Code of Hammurabi says, 'An eye for an eye'.
>
> Proposition に対する自分の立場 (Pro or Con) の主張とその論拠を述べる。必要か不要かの主張をし、自分がそう考える理由を述べる。
> ・The death penalty is not needed in Japan, because capital punishment is murder.
> ・Capital punishment is needed in Japan, because it prevents crime.
>
> ◀ **Body**
> **-Reason**
> **-Evidence**
>
> その理由をサポートする論拠 (Evidence) を例や数字で示す。
> ・According to the statistics, … (データ)
> ・In 1992, there was a murder case … (実例)
> ・The Universal Declaration of Human Rights says … (引用)
>
> 繰り返しとまとめ、締めの言葉
> ・Therefore, I think we need ….
> ・From the above, capital punishment should be…
> ・All life is precious and we should never be allowed to kill other people.
> ・In order to keep our society safe, we need capital punishment.
>
> ◀ **Conclusion**

Peer Editing

Exchange your drafts and correct errors if any. Make comments to improve your partner's speech.

Evaluation form 1

The speaker: _____

The title: _____

5: very much agree   4: agree   3: so so   2: don't think so   1: not at all

(1)	The speaker spoke clearly.	5 4 3 2 1
(2)	The speaker kept good time.	5 4 3 2 1
(3)	The speaker had good eye contact.	5 4 3 2 1
(4)	The speaker used good visual aids.	5 4 3 2 1
(5)	The content of the speech was interesting.	5 4 3 2 1

summary

Name _____

The speaker: _____

The title: _____

5: very much agree   4: agree   3: so so   2: don't think so   1: not at all

(1)	The speaker spoke clearly.	5 4 3 2 1
(2)	The speaker kept good time.	5 4 3 2 1
(3)	The speaker had good eye contact.	5 4 3 2 1
(4)	The speaker used good visual aids.	5 4 3 2 1
(5)	The content of the speech was interesting.	5 4 3 2 1

summary

Name _____

Evaluation form 2
Presenter Evaluation Sheet (students → students)　聴衆用ワークシート

---

example
Presentation evaluation (Students)
Presenter: _Mika_
title: _My future dream_
One point advice:
voice _大きくてよく聞こえたが少し早い。_
eye contact _前半は良かった。後半が少し残念。_
gesture/ posture _頭をかく癖に注意！_
content: _わかりやすくまとまっていた。_
visual aids: _パワーポイントがとても役立った。_
comment: _I feel your dream will come true because your plans sounded very practical._
　　　　　　　　　　　　　From **Yumi**

Presentation evaluation (Students)
Presenter:_____
title:_____
One point advice:
voice _____
eye contact _____
gesture/ posture _____
content: _____
visual aids: _____
comment: _____
_____
　　　　　　　　　　　　　From

Presentation evaluation (Students)
Presenter:_____
title:_____
One point advice:
voice _____
eye contact _____
gesture/ posture _____
content: _____
visual aids: _____
comment: _____
_____
　　　　　　　　　　　　　From

Presentation evaluation (Students)
Presenter:_____
title:_____
One point advice:
voice _____
eye contact _____
gesture/ posture _____
content: _____
visual aids: _____
comment: _____
_____
　　　　　　　　　　　　　From

Presentation evaluation (Students)
Presenter:_____
title:_____
One point advice:
voice _____
eye contact _____
gesture/ posture _____
content: _____
visual aids: _____
comment: _____
_____
　　　　　　　　　　　　　From

Presentation evaluation (Students)
Presenter:_____
title:_____
One point advice:
voice _____
eye contact _____
gesture/ posture _____
content: _____
visual aids: _____
comment: _____
_____
　　　　　　　　　　　　　From

Evaluation form 3

Name of the speaker	Voice & Intonation	Eye contact	Posture & Gestures	Points clearly stated	Attractive content	Fluency	Use of visuals	Your comment
Kei	○	✔	△	○	○	×	○	I liked his humor.

Evaluation form 4

Comparing Rival Companies: In-group & class presentation

groups	names	companies compared	differences	speech (5)	intersts (5)	presenter of the group (✓)
1						
2						
3						
4						
5						
selected	1					
	2					
	3					
	4					
	5					

Evaluation form 5

Student No: Name:

Evaluation Sheet for Poster Presentation

Group: _____
Evaluator's Name: _____

Evaluations	Details	OK (1)	Good (2)	Excellent (3)	Perfect (4)
1. Poster Visual	Impact / Well-organised / Understandable				
2. Presentation Performance	Voice & pacing / Eye-contact / Posture & Gesture				
3. Contents	Informative / Impressive / Persuasive				
Comments					
TOTAL Scores:					/12

Evaluation Sheet for Poster Presentation

Group: _____
Evaluator's Name: _____

Evaluations	Details	OK (1)	Good (2)	Excellent (3)	Perfect (4)
1. Poster Visual	Impact / Well-organised / Understandable				
2. Presentation Performance	Voice & pacing / Eye-contact / Posture & Gesture				
3. Contents	Informative / Impressive / Persuasive				
Comments					
TOTAL Scores:					/12

PREPARE YOUR SPEECH AND PRESENTATION
プレゼンテーションで学ぶ英語4技能

2018年10月1日　初版発行

著者
吉久保肇子（よしくぼ　はつこ）
池尾　玲子（いけお　れいこ）
藤田　玲子（ふじた　れいこ）
山形　亜子（やまがた　あこ）
三浦　愛香（みうら　あいか）

Copyright © 2018 by Hatsuko Yoshikubo, Reiko Ikeo, Reiko Fujita, Ako Yamagata, Aika Miura

KENKYUSHA
〈検印省略〉

発行者　関戸雅男
発行所　株式会社 研究社
　　　　〒102-8152 東京都千代田区富士見 2-11-3
　　　電話　営業 03-3288-7777（代）　編集 03-3288-7711（代）
　　　振替　00150-9-26710
　　　http://www.kenkyusha.co.jp/

本文組版・デザイン　株式会社 明昌堂
本文イラスト　中嶋麻美
印刷所　研究社印刷株式会社
音声吹き込み　Chris Koprowski, Jessica Kozuka
音声録音・編集　（株）東京録音

ISBN 978-4-327-42199-1　C1082　　Printed in Japan

本書の無断複写（コピー）は著作権法上での例外を除き、禁じられています。
また、私的使用以外のいかなる電子的複製行為も一切認められておりません。
落丁本・乱丁本はお取り替えいたします。ただし、古書店で購入したものについてはお取り替えできません。